THE COMPLETE HOMESCHOOL

PLANNER AND JOURNAL

A 180-Day Record Book
for Homeschoolers and Involved Parents

LARRY ZAFRAN

Self-published by Author

THE COMPLETE HOMESCHOOL PLANNER AND JOURNAL
A 180-Day Record Book for Homeschoolers and Involved Parents

VShane Studio
www.vshane-art.com
Designed and illustrated the cover
Graphic illustrator and designer since 1995
Contemporary, Main Stream, B2B and B2C

Printed in the United States of America
First Edition printing May 2011

ISBN-10: 1-4610-8494-6
ISBN-13: 978-1-46-108494-5

www.LarryZafran.com

HOW TO USE THIS BOOK

This book provides space for 180 days of comprehensive homeschool planner/journal entries. They are self-explanatory and adaptable for homeschoolers or involved parents who are tracking or supplementing the education of traditional school students. The book includes an attendance calendar, forms to document the syllabus/textbooks/materials for each subject, and fields to document other pieces of information which may be requested and/or required by government or school officials.

The point of homeschooling is that every child and his/her educational needs are unique. With that in mind, parents should utilize and adapt this book as they feel is best. One suggestion is to use future daily entries for advance planning. As those days arrive, the *Notes* field for each subject can be notated with a checkmark if all went according to plan, or can be used to notate topics that weren't fully covered or need to be revisited later.

ABOUT THE AUTHOR AND COMPANION WEBSITE

Larry Zafran was born and raised in Queens, NY where he tutored and taught math in public and private schools. He has a Bachelors Degree in Computer Science from Queens College, and most of the credits toward a Masters Degree in Secondary Math Education. He is a dedicated student of the piano, and the leader of a large and active group of board game players that focuses on strategy games from Europe. He lives with his fiancée in Cary, NC where he works as an independent math tutor, writer, and webmaster. Please visit **www.LarryZafran.com** for information about the author's published and upcoming books, or to discuss this book, or to download additional printable pages at no cost.

ALSO BY THE AUTHOR

WEIGHT LOSS MADE A BIT EASIER:
Realistic and Practical Advice
for Healthy Eating and Exercise

A REALISTIC EATING AND EXERCISE
RECORD BOOK: A Six-Month Weight Loss Log
and Journal for Dedicated Individuals

THE COMPLETE MUSIC PRACTICE RECORD
BOOK: A Six-Month Log and Journal
for Dedicated Students

AMERICA'S (MATH) EDUCATION CRISIS:
Why We Have It and Why We Can('t) Fix It

THE REGIFTABLE GIFT BOOK:
The Gift That Keeps On Regiving

MATH MADE A BIT EASIER:
Basic Math Explained in Plain English

MATH MADE A BIT EASIER WORKBOOK:
Practice Exercises, Self-Tests, and Review

MATH MADE A BIT EASIER LESSON PLANS:
A Guide for Tutors, Parents, and Homeschoolers

BASIC ALGEBRA AND GEOMETRY MADE
A BIT EASIER: Concepts Explained in Plain
English, Practice Exercises, and Self-Tests

BASIC ALG./GEOM. M.A.B.E. LESSON PLANS:
A Guide for Tutors, Parents, and Homeschoolers

Additional Titles in These Genres Coming Soon

STUDENT AND PARENT INFORMATION

Student's Name: _____
Parents' Names: _____
Address:_____
Address:_____
e-Mail: _____
Phone: _____
Misc. Info: _____

MISC. INFORMATION, IMMUNIZATION RECORDS

_____
_____
_____
_____
_____
_____
_____

UPCOMING EXAMS AND SPECIAL EVENTS

_____
_____
_____
_____
_____
_____
_____

TOTAL CREDITS PER SUBJECT BEFORE/AFTER SEMESTER

_____   _____
_____   _____
_____   _____
_____   _____
_____   _____
_____   _____

LOCAL SCHOOL / DISTRICT INFO.

School/Contact: _____
Address: _____
Address: _____
e-Mail: _____
Website: _____
Phone/Fax: _____
Misc. Info: _____

INSTRUCTOR / TUTOR / HOMESCHOOL CO-OP INFO.

Contact Name:_____
Address: _____
Address: _____
e-Mail: _____
Website: _____
Phone/Fax: _____
Misc. Info:_____

REPORT CARD / COURSE GRADES

_____   _____
_____   _____
_____   _____
_____   _____
_____   _____

· DAILY/WEEKLY INSTRUCTION SCHEDULE

_____   _____
_____   _____
_____   _____
_____   _____
_____   _____
_____   _____

Homeschool Attendance Record
for the School/Calendar Year _____

	Jan	Feb	Mar	Apr	May	Jun	Jul	Aug	Sep	Oct	Nov	Dec
1												
2												
3												
4												
5												
6												
7												
8												
9												
10												
11												
12												
13												
14												
15												
16												
17												
18												
19												
20												
21												
22												
23												
24												
25												
26												
27												
28												
29												
30												
31												
Total												

Symbols/Abbreviations Used:

GENERAL SYLLABUS/CURRICULUM FOR EACH SUBJECT

Reading/Literature: _____

Writing/Language Arts: _____

Mathematics: _____

Science/Lab: _____

US Hist./Govt./Civics:_____

World History/Geography: _____

Foreign Language:_____

Sports/Fitness/Phys. Ed.: _____

Music: _____

Visual Arts:_____

Performing Arts: _____

Religious/Cultural Studies:_____

Field Trips: _____

Trade Skills/Shop:_____

Health/Hygiene/Nutrition: _____

Computers/Tech./Business Skills: _____

Comm. Svc./Volunteerism/Career:_____

Home Economics/Chores: _____

Electives/Hobbies/Clubs:_____

Miscellaneous: _____

TEXTBOOKS/WORKBOOKS/MATERIALS FOR EACH SUBJECT

Reading/Literature: _____

Writing/Language Arts: _____

Mathematics: _____

Science/Lab: _____

US Hist./Govt./Civics: _____

World History/Geography: _____

Foreign Language: _____

Sports/Fitness/Phys. Ed.: _____

Music: _____

Visual Arts: _____

Performing Arts: _____

Religious/Cultural Studies: _____

Field Trips: _____

Trade Skills/Shop: _____

Health/Hygiene/Nutrition: _____

Computers/Tech./Business Skills: _____

Comm. Svc./Volunteerism/Career: _____

Home Economics/Chores: _____

Electives/Hobbies/Clubs: _____

Miscellaneous: _____

Day 1 Date: __ / __ / __ Hours: _____ Admin. Notes: _____

Reading/Literature: _____
Notes: _____
Writing/Language Arts: _____
Notes: _____
Mathematics: _____
Notes: _____
Science/Lab: _____
Notes: _____
US Hist./Govt./Civics: _____
Notes: _____
World History/Geography: _____
Notes: _____
Foreign Language: _____
Notes: _____
Sports/Fitness/Phys. Ed.: _____
Notes: _____
Music: _____
Notes: _____
Visual Arts: _____
Notes: _____
Performing Arts: _____
Notes: _____
Religious/Cultural Studies: _____
Notes: _____
Field Trips: _____
Notes: _____
Trade Skills/Shop: _____
Notes: _____
Health/Hygiene/Nutrition: _____
Notes: _____
Computers/Tech./Business Skills: _____
Notes: _____
Comm. Svc./Volunteerism/Career: _____
Notes: _____
Home Economics/Chores: _____
Notes: _____
Electives/Hobbies/Clubs: _____
Notes: _____
Miscellaneous: _____

Day 2 Date: __ /__ /__ Hours: _____ Admin. Notes: _____

Reading/Literature: _____
Notes: _____

Writing/Language Arts: _____
Notes: _____

Mathematics: _____
Notes: _____

Science/Lab: _____
Notes: _____

US Hist./Govt./Civics: _____
Notes: _____

World History/Geography: _____
Notes: _____

Foreign Language: _____
Notes: _____

Sports/Fitness/Phys. Ed.: _____
Notes: _____

Music: _____
Notes: _____

Visual Arts: _____
Notes: _____

Performing Arts: _____
Notes: _____

Religious/Cultural Studies: _____
Notes: _____

Field Trips: _____
Notes: _____

Trade Skills/Shop: _____
Notes: _____

Health/Hygiene/Nutrition: _____
Notes: _____

Computers/Tech./Business Skills: _____
Notes: _____

Comm. Svc./Volunteerism/Career: _____
Notes: _____

Home Economics/Chores: _____
Notes: _____

Electives/Hobbies/Clubs: _____
Notes: _____

Miscellaneous: _____

Day 3 Date: __ /__ /__ Hours: _____ Admin. Notes: _____

Reading/Literature: _____
Notes: _____

Writing/Language Arts: _____
Notes: _____

Mathematics: _____
Notes: _____

Science/Lab: _____
Notes: _____

US Hist./Govt./Civics: _____
Notes: _____

World History/Geography: _____
Notes: _____

Foreign Language: _____
Notes: _____

Sports/Fitness/Phys. Ed.: _____
Notes: _____

Music: _____
Notes: _____

Visual Arts: _____
Notes: _____

Performing Arts: _____
Notes: _____

Religious/Cultural Studies: _____
Notes: _____

Field Trips: _____
Notes: _____

Trade Skills/Shop: _____
Notes: _____

Health/Hygiene/Nutrition: _____
Notes: _____

Computers/Tech./Business Skills: _____
Notes: _____

Comm. Svc./Volunteerism/Career: _____
Notes: _____

Home Economics/Chores: _____
Notes: _____

Electives/Hobbies/Clubs: _____
Notes: _____

Miscellaneous: _____

Day 4 Date: __ /__ /__ Hours: _____ Admin. Notes: _____

Reading/Literature: _____
    Notes: _____

Writing/Language Arts: _____
    Notes: _____

Mathematics: _____
    Notes: _____

Science/Lab: _____
    Notes: _____

US Hist./Govt./Civics: _____
    Notes: _____

World History/Geography: _____
    Notes: _____

Foreign Language: _____
    Notes: _____

Sports/Fitness/Phys. Ed.: _____
    Notes: _____

Music: _____
    Notes: _____

Visual Arts: _____
    Notes: _____

Performing Arts: _____
    Notes: _____

Religious/Cultural Studies: _____
    Notes: _____

Field Trips: _____
    Notes: _____

Trade Skills/Shop: _____
    Notes: _____

Health/Hygiene/Nutrition: _____
    Notes: _____

Computers/Tech./Business Skills: _____
    Notes: _____

Comm. Svc./Volunteerism/Career: _____
    Notes: _____

Home Economics/Chores: _____
    Notes: _____

Electives/Hobbies/Clubs: _____
    Notes: _____

Miscellaneous: _____
_____

Day 5   Date: __ /__ /__   Hours: _____   Admin. Notes: _____

Reading/Literature: _____
Notes: _____

Writing/Language Arts: _____
Notes: _____

Mathematics: _____
Notes: _____

Science/Lab: _____
Notes: _____

US Hist./Govt./Civics: _____
Notes: _____

World History/Geography: _____
Notes: _____

Foreign Language: _____
Notes: _____

Sports/Fitness/Phys. Ed.: _____
Notes: _____

Music: _____
Notes: _____

Visual Arts: _____
Notes: _____

Performing Arts: _____
Notes: _____

Religious/Cultural Studies: _____
Notes: _____

Field Trips: _____
Notes: _____

Trade Skills/Shop: _____
Notes: _____

Health/Hygiene/Nutrition: _____
Notes: _____

Computers/Tech./Business Skills: _____
Notes: _____

Comm. Svc./Volunteerism/Career: _____
Notes: _____

Home Economics/Chores: _____
Notes: _____

Electives/Hobbies/Clubs: _____
Notes: _____

Miscellaneous: _____

Day 6 Date: __ /__ /__ Hours: _____ Admin. Notes: _____

Reading/Literature: _____
Notes: _____

Writing/Language Arts: _____
Notes: _____

Mathematics: _____
Notes: _____

Science/Lab: _____
Notes: _____

US Hist./Govt./Civics: _____
Notes: _____

World History/Geography: _____
Notes: _____

Foreign Language: _____
Notes: _____

Sports/Fitness/Phys. Ed.: _____
Notes: _____

Music: _____
Notes: _____

Visual Arts: _____
Notes: _____

Performing Arts: _____
Notes: _____

Religious/Cultural Studies: _____
Notes: _____

Field Trips: _____
Notes: _____

Trade Skills/Shop: _____
Notes: _____

Health/Hygiene/Nutrition: _____
Notes: _____

Computers/Tech./Business Skills: _____
Notes: _____

Comm. Svc./Volunteerism/Career: _____
Notes: _____

Home Economics/Chores: _____
Notes: _____

Electives/Hobbies/Clubs: _____
Notes: _____

Miscellaneous: _____
_____

Day 7 Date: __ /__ /__ Hours: _____ Admin. Notes: _____

Reading/Literature: _____
Notes: _____

Writing/Language Arts: _____
Notes: _____

Mathematics: _____
Notes: _____

Science/Lab: _____
Notes: _____

US Hist./Govt./Civics: _____
Notes: _____

World History/Geography: _____
Notes: _____

Foreign Language: _____
Notes: _____

Sports/Fitness/Phys. Ed.: _____
Notes: _____

Music: _____
Notes: _____

Visual Arts: _____
Notes: _____

Performing Arts: _____
Notes: _____

Religious/Cultural Studies: _____
Notes: _____

Field Trips: _____
Notes: _____

Trade Skills/Shop: _____
Notes: _____

Health/Hygiene/Nutrition: _____
Notes: _____

Computers/Tech./Business Skills: _____
Notes: _____

Comm. Svc./Volunteerism/Career: _____
Notes: _____

Home Economics/Chores: _____
Notes: _____

Electives/Hobbies/Clubs: _____
Notes: _____

Miscellaneous: _____

Day 8   Date: __ /__ /__   Hours: _____   Admin. Notes: _____

Reading/Literature: _____
   Notes: _____

Writing/Language Arts: _____
   Notes: _____

Mathematics: _____
   Notes: _____

Science/Lab: _____
   Notes: _____

US Hist./Govt./Civics: _____
   Notes: _____

World History/Geography: _____
   Notes: _____

Foreign Language: _____
   Notes: _____

Sports/Fitness/Phys. Ed.: _____
   Notes: _____

Music: _____
   Notes: _____

Visual Arts: _____
   Notes: _____

Performing Arts: _____
   Notes: _____

Religious/Cultural Studies: _____
   Notes: _____

Field Trips: _____
   Notes: _____

Trade Skills/Shop: _____
   Notes: _____

Health/Hygiene/Nutrition: _____
   Notes: _____

Computers/Tech./Business Skills: _____
   Notes: _____

Comm. Svc./Volunteerism/Career: _____
   Notes: _____

Home Economics/Chores: _____
   Notes: _____

Electives/Hobbies/Clubs: _____
   Notes: _____

Miscellaneous: _____
_____

Day 9 Date: __ /__ /__ Hours: _____ Admin. Notes: _____

Reading/Literature: _____
Notes: _____

Writing/Language Arts: _____
Notes: _____

Mathematics: _____
Notes: _____

Science/Lab: _____
Notes: _____

US Hist./Govt./Civics: _____
Notes: _____

World History/Geography: _____
Notes: _____

Foreign Language: _____
Notes: _____

Sports/Fitness/Phys. Ed.: _____
Notes: _____

Music: _____
Notes: _____

Visual Arts: _____
Notes: _____

Performing Arts: _____
Notes: _____

Religious/Cultural Studies: _____
Notes: _____

Field Trips: _____
Notes: _____

Trade Skills/Shop: _____
Notes: _____

Health/Hygiene/Nutrition: _____
Notes: _____

Computers/Tech./Business Skills: _____
Notes: _____

Comm. Svc./Volunteerism/Career: _____
Notes: _____

Home Economics/Chores: _____
Notes: _____

Electives/Hobbies/Clubs: _____
Notes: _____

Miscellaneous: _____
_____

THE COMPLETE HOMESCHOOL PLANNER AND JOURNAL:
A 180-DAY RECORD BOOK FOR HOMESCHOOLERS AND INVOLVED PARENTS

Day 10   Date: __ /__ /__   Hours: _____   Admin. Notes: _____

Reading/Literature: _____
Notes: _____
Writing/Language Arts: _____
Notes: _____
Mathematics: _____
Notes: _____
Science/Lab: _____
Notes: _____
US Hist./Govt./Civics: _____
Notes: _____
World History/Geography: _____
Notes: _____
Foreign Language: _____
Notes: _____
Sports/Fitness/Phys. Ed.: _____
Notes: _____
Music: _____
Notes: _____
Visual Arts: _____
Notes: _____
Performing Arts: _____
Notes: _____
Religious/Cultural Studies: _____
Notes: _____
Field Trips: _____
Notes: _____
Trade Skills/Shop: _____
Notes: _____
Health/Hygiene/Nutrition: _____
Notes: _____
Computers/Tech./Business Skills: _____
Notes: _____
Comm. Svc./Volunteerism/Career: _____
Notes: _____
Home Economics/Chores: _____
Notes: _____
Electives/Hobbies/Clubs: _____
Notes: _____
Miscellaneous: _____

Day 11   Date: __ / __ / __   Hours: _____   Admin. Notes: _____

Reading/Literature: _____
Notes: _____
Writing/Language Arts: _____
Notes: _____
Mathematics: _____
Notes: _____
Science/Lab: _____
Notes: _____
US Hist./Govt./Civics: _____
Notes: _____
World History/Geography: _____
Notes: _____
Foreign Language: _____
Notes: _____
Sports/Fitness/Phys. Ed.: _____
Notes: _____
Music: _____
Notes: _____
Visual Arts: _____
Notes: _____
Performing Arts: _____
Notes: _____
Religious/Cultural Studies: _____
Notes: _____
Field Trips: _____
Notes: _____
Trade Skills/Shop: _____
Notes: _____
Health/Hygiene/Nutrition: _____
Notes: _____
Computers/Tech./Business Skills: _____
Notes: _____
Comm. Svc./Volunteerism/Career: _____
Notes: _____
Home Economics/Chores: _____
Notes: _____
Electives/Hobbies/Clubs: _____
Notes: _____
Miscellaneous: _____

Day 12 Date: __ /__ /__ Hours: _____ Admin. Notes: _____

Reading/Literature: _____
    Notes: _____

Writing/Language Arts: _____
    Notes: _____

Mathematics: _____
    Notes: _____

Science/Lab: _____
    Notes: _____

US Hist./Govt./Civics: _____
    Notes: _____

World History/Geography: _____
    Notes: _____

Foreign Language: _____
    Notes: _____

Sports/Fitness/Phys. Ed.: _____
    Notes: _____

Music: _____
    Notes: _____

Visual Arts: _____
    Notes: _____

Performing Arts: _____
    Notes: _____

Religious/Cultural Studies: _____
    Notes: _____

Field Trips: _____
    Notes: _____

Trade Skills/Shop: _____
    Notes: _____

Health/Hygiene/Nutrition: _____
    Notes: _____

Computers/Tech./Business Skills: _____
    Notes: _____

Comm. Svc./Volunteerism/Career: _____
    Notes: _____

Home Economics/Chores: _____
    Notes: _____

Electives/Hobbies/Clubs: _____
    Notes: _____

Miscellaneous: _____
_____

Day 13   Date: __ /__ /__   Hours: _____   Admin. Notes: _____

Reading/Literature: _____
   Notes: _____
Writing/Language Arts: _____
   Notes: _____
Mathematics: _____
   Notes: _____
Science/Lab: _____
   Notes: _____
US Hist./Govt./Civics: _____
   Notes: _____
World History/Geography: _____
   Notes: _____
Foreign Language: _____
   Notes: _____
Sports/Fitness/Phys. Ed.: _____
   Notes: _____
Music: _____
   Notes: _____
Visual Arts: _____
   Notes: _____
Performing Arts: _____
   Notes: _____
Religious/Cultural Studies: _____
   Notes: _____
Field Trips: _____
   Notes: _____
Trade Skills/Shop: _____
   Notes: _____
Health/Hygiene/Nutrition: _____
   Notes: _____
Computers/Tech./Business Skills: _____
   Notes: _____
Comm. Svc./Volunteerism/Career: _____
   Notes: _____
Home Economics/Chores: _____
   Notes: _____
Electives/Hobbies/Clubs: _____
   Notes: _____
Miscellaneous: _____
_____

Day 14   Date: __ /__ /__   Hours: _____   Admin. Notes: _____

Reading/Literature: _____
   Notes: _____

Writing/Language Arts: _____
   Notes: _____

Mathematics: _____
   Notes: _____

Science/Lab: _____
   Notes: _____

US Hist./Govt./Civics: _____
   Notes: _____

World History/Geography: _____
   Notes: _____

Foreign Language: _____
   Notes: _____

Sports/Fitness/Phys. Ed.: _____
   Notes: _____

Music: _____
   Notes: _____

Visual Arts: _____
   Notes: _____

Performing Arts: _____
   Notes: _____

Religious/Cultural Studies: _____
   Notes: _____

Field Trips: _____
   Notes: _____

Trade Skills/Shop: _____
   Notes: _____

Health/Hygiene/Nutrition: _____
   Notes: _____

Computers/Tech./Business Skills: _____
   Notes: _____

Comm. Svc./Volunteerism/Career: _____
   Notes: _____

Home Economics/Chores: _____
   Notes: _____

Electives/Hobbies/Clubs: _____
   Notes: _____

Miscellaneous: _____
_____

Day 15 Date: __ /__ /__ Hours: _____ Admin. Notes: _____

Reading/Literature: _____
Notes: _____

Writing/Language Arts: _____
Notes: _____

Mathematics: _____
Notes: _____

Science/Lab: _____
Notes: _____

US Hist./Govt./Civics: _____
Notes: _____

World History/Geography: _____
Notes: _____

Foreign Language: _____
Notes: _____

Sports/Fitness/Phys. Ed.: _____
Notes: _____

Music: _____
Notes: _____

Visual Arts: _____
Notes: _____

Performing Arts: _____
Notes: _____

Religious/Cultural Studies: _____
Notes: _____

Field Trips: _____
Notes: _____

Trade Skills/Shop: _____
Notes: _____

Health/Hygiene/Nutrition: _____
Notes: _____

Computers/Tech./Business Skills: _____
Notes: _____

Comm. Svc./Volunteerism/Career: _____
Notes: _____

Home Economics/Chores: _____
Notes: _____

Electives/Hobbies/Clubs: _____
Notes: _____

Miscellaneous: _____

Day 16   Date: __ / __ / __   Hours: _____   Admin. Notes: _____

Reading/Literature: _____
   Notes: _____

Writing/Language Arts: _____
   Notes: _____

Mathematics: _____
   Notes: _____

Science/Lab: _____
   Notes: _____

US Hist./Govt./Civics: _____
   Notes: _____

World History/Geography: _____
   Notes: _____

Foreign Language: _____
   Notes: _____

Sports/Fitness/Phys. Ed.: _____
   Notes: _____

Music: _____
   Notes: _____

Visual Arts: _____
   Notes: _____

Performing Arts: _____
   Notes: _____

Religious/Cultural Studies: _____
   Notes: _____

Field Trips: _____
   Notes: _____

Trade Skills/Shop: _____
   Notes: _____

Health/Hygiene/Nutrition: _____
   Notes: _____

Computers/Tech./Business Skills: _____
   Notes: _____

Comm. Svc./Volunteerism/Career: _____
   Notes: _____

Home Economics/Chores: _____
   Notes: _____

Electives/Hobbies/Clubs: _____
   Notes: _____

Miscellaneous: _____
_____

Day 17 Date: __ /__ /__ **Hours:** _____ **Admin. Notes:** _____

Reading/Literature: _____
Notes: _____

Writing/Language Arts: _____
Notes: _____

Mathematics: _____
Notes: _____

Science/Lab: _____
Notes: _____

US Hist./Govt./Civics: _____
Notes: _____

World History/Geography: _____
Notes: _____

Foreign Language: _____
Notes: _____

Sports/Fitness/Phys. Ed.: _____
Notes: _____

Music: _____
Notes: _____

Visual Arts: _____
Notes: _____

Performing Arts: _____
Notes: _____

Religious/Cultural Studies: _____
Notes: _____

Field Trips: _____
Notes: _____

Trade Skills/Shop: _____
Notes: _____

Health/Hygiene/Nutrition: _____
Notes: _____

Computers/Tech./Business Skills: _____
Notes: _____

Comm. Svc./Volunteerism/Career: _____
Notes: _____

Home Economics/Chores: _____
Notes: _____

Electives/Hobbies/Clubs: _____
Notes: _____

Miscellaneous: _____
_____

Day 18 Date: __ /__ /__ Hours: _____ Admin. Notes: _____

Reading/Literature: _____
　　Notes: _____

Writing/Language Arts: _____
　　Notes: _____

Mathematics: _____
　　Notes: _____

Science/Lab: _____
　　Notes: _____

US Hist./Govt./Civics: _____
　　Notes: _____

World History/Geography: _____
　　Notes: _____

Foreign Language: _____
　　Notes: _____

Sports/Fitness/Phys. Ed.: _____
　　Notes: _____

Music: _____
　　Notes: _____

Visual Arts: _____
　　Notes: _____

Performing Arts: _____
　　Notes: _____

Religious/Cultural Studies: _____
　　Notes: _____

Field Trips: _____
　　Notes: _____

Trade Skills/Shop: _____
　　Notes: _____

Health/Hygiene/Nutrition: _____
　　Notes: _____

Computers/Tech./Business Skills: _____
　　Notes: _____

Comm. Svc./Volunteerism/Career: _____
　　Notes: _____

Home Economics/Chores: _____
　　Notes: _____

Electives/Hobbies/Clubs: _____
　　Notes: _____

Miscellaneous: _____
_____

Day 19   Date: __ / __ / __   Hours: _____   Admin. Notes: _____

Reading/Literature: _____
Notes: _____

Writing/Language Arts: _____
Notes: _____

Mathematics: _____
Notes: _____

Science/Lab: _____
Notes: _____

US Hist./Govt./Civics: _____
Notes: _____

World History/Geography: _____
Notes: _____

Foreign Language: _____
Notes: _____

Sports/Fitness/Phys. Ed.: _____
Notes: _____

Music: _____
Notes: _____

Visual Arts: _____
Notes: _____

Performing Arts: _____
Notes: _____

Religious/Cultural Studies: _____
Notes: _____

Field Trips: _____
Notes: _____

Trade Skills/Shop: _____
Notes: _____

Health/Hygiene/Nutrition: _____
Notes: _____

Computers/Tech./Business Skills: _____
Notes: _____

Comm. Svc./Volunteerism/Career: _____
Notes: _____

Home Economics/Chores: _____
Notes: _____

Electives/Hobbies/Clubs: _____
Notes: _____

Miscellaneous: _____
_____

Day 20   Date: __ /__ /__   Hours: _____   Admin. Notes: _____

Reading/Literature: _____
  Notes: _____

Writing/Language Arts: _____
  Notes: _____

Mathematics: _____
  Notes: _____

Science/Lab: _____
  Notes: _____

US Hist./Govt./Civics: _____
  Notes: _____

World History/Geography: _____
  Notes: _____

Foreign Language: _____
  Notes: _____

Sports/Fitness/Phys. Ed.: _____
  Notes: _____

Music: _____
  Notes: _____

Visual Arts: _____
  Notes: _____

Performing Arts: _____
  Notes: _____

Religious/Cultural Studies: _____
  Notes: _____

Field Trips: _____
  Notes: _____

Trade Skills/Shop: _____
  Notes: _____

Health/Hygiene/Nutrition: _____
  Notes: _____

Computers/Tech./Business Skills: _____
  Notes: _____

Comm. Svc./Volunteerism/Career: _____
  Notes: _____

Home Economics/Chores: _____
  Notes: _____

Electives/Hobbies/Clubs: _____
  Notes: _____

Miscellaneous: _____
_____

Day 21 Date: __ /__ /__ Hours: _____ Admin. Notes:_____

Reading/Literature: _____
   Notes: _____

Writing/Language Arts: _____
   Notes: _____

Mathematics: _____
   Notes: _____

Science/Lab: _____
   Notes: _____

US Hist./Govt./Civics: _____
   Notes: _____

World History/Geography: _____
   Notes: _____

Foreign Language: _____
   Notes: _____

Sports/Fitness/Phys. Ed.: _____
   Notes: _____

Music: _____
   Notes: _____

Visual Arts: _____
   Notes: _____

Performing Arts: _____
   Notes: _____

Religious/Cultural Studies: _____
   Notes: _____

Field Trips: _____
   Notes: _____

Trade Skills/Shop: _____
   Notes: _____

Health/Hygiene/Nutrition: _____
   Notes: _____

Computers/Tech./Business Skills: _____
   Notes: _____

Comm. Svc./Volunteerism/Career: _____
   Notes: _____

Home Economics/Chores: _____
   Notes: _____

Electives/Hobbies/Clubs: _____
   Notes: _____

Miscellaneous: _____

Day 22 Date: __ /__ /__ Hours: _____ Admin. Notes: _____

Reading/Literature: _____
Notes: _____

Writing/Language Arts: _____
Notes: _____

Mathematics: _____
Notes: _____

Science/Lab: _____
Notes: _____

US Hist./Govt./Civics: _____
Notes: _____

World History/Geography: _____
Notes: _____

Foreign Language: _____
Notes: _____

Sports/Fitness/Phys. Ed.: _____
Notes: _____

Music: _____
Notes: _____

Visual Arts: _____
Notes: _____

Performing Arts: _____
Notes: _____

Religious/Cultural Studies: _____
Notes: _____

Field Trips: _____
Notes: _____

Trade Skills/Shop: _____
Notes: _____

Health/Hygiene/Nutrition: _____
Notes: _____

Computers/Tech./Business Skills: _____
Notes: _____

Comm. Svc./Volunteerism/Career: _____
Notes: _____

Home Economics/Chores: _____
Notes: _____

Electives/Hobbies/Clubs: _____
Notes: _____

Miscellaneous: _____
_____

Day 23 Date: __ / __ / __ Hours: _____ Admin. Notes: _____

Reading/Literature: _____
   Notes: _____

Writing/Language Arts: _____
   Notes: _____

Mathematics: _____
   Notes: _____

Science/Lab: _____
   Notes: _____

US Hist./Govt./Civics: _____
   Notes: _____

World History/Geography: _____
   Notes: _____

Foreign Language: _____
   Notes: _____

Sports/Fitness/Phys. Ed.: _____
   Notes: _____

Music: _____
   Notes: _____

Visual Arts: _____
   Notes: _____

Performing Arts: _____
   Notes: _____

Religious/Cultural Studies: _____
   Notes: _____

Field Trips: _____
   Notes: _____

Trade Skills/Shop: _____
   Notes: _____

Health/Hygiene/Nutrition: _____
   Notes: _____

Computers/Tech./Business Skills: _____
   Notes: _____

Comm. Svc./Volunteerism/Career: _____
   Notes: _____

Home Economics/Chores: _____
   Notes: _____

Electives/Hobbies/Clubs: _____
   Notes: _____

Miscellaneous: _____
_____

Day 24 Date: __ /__ /__ Hours: _____ Admin. Notes: _____

Reading/Literature: _____
   Notes: _____
Writing/Language Arts: _____
   Notes: _____
Mathematics: _____
   Notes: _____
Science/Lab: _____
   Notes: _____
US Hist./Govt./Civics: _____
   Notes: _____
World History/Geography: _____
   Notes: _____
Foreign Language: _____
   Notes: _____
Sports/Fitness/Phys. Ed.: _____
   Notes: _____
Music: _____
   Notes: _____
Visual Arts: _____
   Notes: _____
Performing Arts: _____
   Notes: _____
Religious/Cultural Studies: _____
   Notes: _____
Field Trips: _____
   Notes: _____
Trade Skills/Shop: _____
   Notes: _____
Health/Hygiene/Nutrition: _____
   Notes: _____
Computers/Tech./Business Skills: _____
   Notes: _____
Comm. Svc./Volunteerism/Career: _____
   Notes: _____
Home Economics/Chores: _____
   Notes: _____
Electives/Hobbies/Clubs: _____
   Notes: _____
Miscellaneous: _____
_____

Day 25 Date: __ /__ /__ Hours: _____ Admin. Notes: _____

Reading/Literature: _____
Notes: _____

Writing/Language Arts: _____
Notes: _____

Mathematics: _____
Notes: _____

Science/Lab: _____
Notes: _____

US Hist./Govt./Civics: _____
Notes: _____

World History/Geography: _____
Notes: _____

Foreign Language: _____
Notes: _____

Sports/Fitness/Phys. Ed.: _____
Notes: _____

Music: _____
Notes: _____

Visual Arts: _____
Notes: _____

Performing Arts: _____
Notes: _____

Religious/Cultural Studies: _____
Notes: _____

Field Trips: _____
Notes: _____

Trade Skills/Shop: _____
Notes: _____

Health/Hygiene/Nutrition: _____
Notes: _____

Computers/Tech./Business Skills: _____
Notes: _____

Comm. Svc./Volunteerism/Career: _____
Notes: _____

Home Economics/Chores: _____
Notes: _____

Electives/Hobbies/Clubs: _____
Notes: _____

Miscellaneous: _____

Day 26   Date: __ /__ /__   Hours: _____   Admin. Notes: _____

Reading/Literature: _____
   Notes: _____

Writing/Language Arts: _____
   Notes: _____

Mathematics: _____
   Notes: _____

Science/Lab: _____
   Notes: _____

US Hist./Govt./Civics: _____
   Notes: _____

World History/Geography: _____
   Notes: _____

Foreign Language: _____
   Notes: _____

Sports/Fitness/Phys. Ed.: _____
   Notes: _____

Music: _____
   Notes: _____

Visual Arts: _____
   Notes: _____

Performing Arts: _____
   Notes: _____

Religious/Cultural Studies: _____
   Notes: _____

Field Trips: _____
   Notes: _____

Trade Skills/Shop: _____
   Notes: _____

Health/Hygiene/Nutrition: _____
   Notes: _____

Computers/Tech./Business Skills: _____
   Notes: _____

Comm. Svc./Volunteerism/Career: _____
   Notes: _____

Home Economics/Chores: _____
   Notes: _____

Electives/Hobbies/Clubs: _____
   Notes: _____

Miscellaneous: _____
_____

Day 27   Date: __ / __ / __   Hours: _____   Admin. Notes: _____

Reading/Literature: _____
  Notes: _____

Writing/Language Arts: _____
  Notes: _____

Mathematics: _____
  Notes: _____

Science/Lab: _____
  Notes: _____

US Hist./Govt./Civics: _____
  Notes: _____

World History/Geography: _____
  Notes: _____

Foreign Language: _____
  Notes: _____

Sports/Fitness/Phys. Ed.: _____
  Notes: _____

Music: _____
  Notes: _____

Visual Arts: _____
  Notes: _____

Performing Arts: _____
  Notes: _____

Religious/Cultural Studies: _____
  Notes: _____

Field Trips: _____
  Notes: _____

Trade Skills/Shop: _____
  Notes: _____

Health/Hygiene/Nutrition: _____
  Notes: _____

Computers/Tech./Business Skills: _____
  Notes: _____

Comm. Svc./Volunteerism/Career: _____
  Notes: _____

Home Economics/Chores: _____
  Notes: _____

Electives/Hobbies/Clubs: _____
  Notes: _____

Miscellaneous: _____

Day 28   Date: __ /__ /__   Hours: _____   Admin. Notes: _____

Reading/Literature: _____
   Notes: _____

Writing/Language Arts: _____
   Notes: _____

Mathematics: _____
   Notes: _____

Science/Lab: _____
   Notes: _____

US Hist./Govt./Civics: _____
   Notes: _____

World History/Geography: _____
   Notes: _____

Foreign Language: _____
   Notes: _____

Sports/Fitness/Phys. Ed.: _____
   Notes: _____

Music: _____
   Notes: _____

Visual Arts: _____
   Notes: _____

Performing Arts: _____
   Notes: _____

Religious/Cultural Studies: _____
   Notes: _____

Field Trips: _____
   Notes: _____

Trade Skills/Shop: _____
   Notes: _____

Health/Hygiene/Nutrition: _____
   Notes: _____

Computers/Tech./Business Skills: _____
   Notes: _____

Comm. Svc./Volunteerism/Career: _____
   Notes: _____

Home Economics/Chores: _____
   Notes: _____

Electives/Hobbies/Clubs: _____
   Notes: _____

Miscellaneous: _____

Day 29 Date: __ /__ /__ Hours: _____ Admin. Notes: _____

Reading/Literature: _____
Notes: _____

Writing/Language Arts: _____
Notes: _____

Mathematics: _____
Notes: _____

Science/Lab: _____
Notes: _____

US Hist./Govt./Civics: _____
Notes: _____

World History/Geography: _____
Notes: _____

Foreign Language: _____
Notes: _____

Sports/Fitness/Phys. Ed.: _____
Notes: _____

Music: _____
Notes: _____

Visual Arts: _____
Notes: _____

Performing Arts: _____
Notes: _____

Religious/Cultural Studies: _____
Notes: _____

Field Trips: _____
Notes: _____

Trade Skills/Shop: _____
Notes: _____

Health/Hygiene/Nutrition: _____
Notes: _____

Computers/Tech./Business Skills: _____
Notes: _____

Comm. Svc./Volunteerism/Career: _____
Notes: _____

Home Economics/Chores: _____
Notes: _____

Electives/Hobbies/Clubs: _____
Notes: _____

Miscellaneous: _____
_____

Day 30 Date: __ /__ /__ Hours: _____ Admin. Notes: _____

Reading/Literature: _____
Notes: _____
Writing/Language Arts: _____
Notes: _____
Mathematics: _____
Notes: _____
Science/Lab: _____
Notes: _____
US Hist./Govt./Civics: _____
Notes: _____
World History/Geography: _____
Notes: _____
Foreign Language: _____
Notes: _____
Sports/Fitness/Phys. Ed.: _____
Notes: _____
Music: _____
Notes: _____
Visual Arts: _____
Notes: _____
Performing Arts: _____
Notes: _____
Religious/Cultural Studies: _____
Notes: _____
Field Trips: _____
Notes: _____
Trade Skills/Shop: _____
Notes: _____
Health/Hygiene/Nutrition: _____
Notes: _____
Computers/Tech./Business Skills: _____
Notes: _____
Comm. Svc./Volunteerism/Career: _____
Notes: _____
Home Economics/Chores: _____
Notes: _____
Electives/Hobbies/Clubs: _____
Notes: _____
Miscellaneous: _____
_____

THE COMPLETE HOMESCHOOL PLANNER AND JOURNAL:
A 180-DAY RECORD BOOK FOR HOMESCHOOLERS AND INVOLVED PARENTS

Day 31   Date: __ /__ /__   Hours: _____   Admin. Notes:_____

Reading/Literature: _____
  Notes: _____
Writing/Language Arts: _____
  Notes: _____
Mathematics: _____
  Notes: _____
Science/Lab: _____
  Notes: _____
US Hist./Govt./Civics: _____
  Notes: _____
World History/Geography: _____
  Notes: _____
Foreign Language: _____
  Notes: _____
Sports/Fitness/Phys. Ed.: _____
  Notes: _____
Music: _____
  Notes: _____
Visual Arts: _____
  Notes: _____
Performing Arts: _____
  Notes: _____
Religious/Cultural Studies: _____
  Notes: _____
Field Trips: _____
  Notes: _____
Trade Skills/Shop: _____
  Notes: _____
Health/Hygiene/Nutrition: _____
  Notes: _____
Computers/Tech./Business Skills: _____
  Notes: _____
Comm. Svc./Volunteerism/Career: _____
  Notes: _____
Home Economics/Chores: _____
  Notes: _____
Electives/Hobbies/Clubs: _____
  Notes: _____
Miscellaneous: _____

Day 32 Date: __ /__ /__ Hours: _____ Admin. Notes: _____

Reading/Literature: _____
   Notes: _____

Writing/Language Arts: _____
   Notes: _____

Mathematics: _____
   Notes: _____

Science/Lab: _____
   Notes: _____

US Hist./Govt./Civics: _____
   Notes: _____

World History/Geography: _____
   Notes: _____

Foreign Language: _____
   Notes: _____

Sports/Fitness/Phys. Ed.: _____
   Notes: _____

Music: _____
   Notes: _____

Visual Arts: _____
   Notes: _____

Performing Arts: _____
   Notes: _____

Religious/Cultural Studies: _____
   Notes: _____

Field Trips: _____
   Notes: _____

Trade Skills/Shop: _____
   Notes: _____

Health/Hygiene/Nutrition: _____
   Notes: _____

Computers/Tech./Business Skills: _____
   Notes: _____

Comm. Svc./Volunteerism/Career: _____
   Notes: _____

Home Economics/Chores: _____
   Notes: _____

Electives/Hobbies/Clubs: _____
   Notes: _____

Miscellaneous: _____
_____

Day 33   Date: __ /__ /__   Hours: _____   Admin. Notes:_____

Reading/Literature: _____
  Notes: _____
Writing/Language Arts: _____
  Notes: _____
Mathematics: _____
  Notes: _____
Science/Lab: _____
  Notes: _____
US Hist./Govt./Civics: _____
  Notes: _____
World History/Geography: _____
  Notes: _____
Foreign Language: _____
  Notes: _____
Sports/Fitness/Phys. Ed.: _____
  Notes: _____
Music: _____
  Notes: _____
Visual Arts: _____
  Notes: _____
Performing Arts: _____
  Notes: _____
Religious/Cultural Studies: _____
  Notes: _____
Field Trips: _____
  Notes: _____
Trade Skills/Shop: _____
  Notes: _____
Health/Hygiene/Nutrition: _____
  Notes: _____
Computers/Tech./Business Skills: _____
  Notes: _____
Comm. Svc./Volunteerism/Career: _____
  Notes: _____
Home Economics/Chores: _____
  Notes: _____
Electives/Hobbies/Clubs: _____
  Notes: _____
Miscellaneous: _____
_____

Day 34 Date: __ /__ /__ Hours: _____ Admin. Notes: _____

Reading/Literature: _____
   Notes: _____

Writing/Language Arts: _____
   Notes: _____

Mathematics: _____
   Notes: _____

Science/Lab: _____
   Notes: _____

US Hist./Govt./Civics:_____
   Notes: _____

World History/Geography: _____
   Notes: _____

Foreign Language:_____
   Notes: _____

Sports/Fitness/Phys. Ed.: _____
   Notes: _____

Music: _____
   Notes: _____

Visual Arts:_____
   Notes: _____

Performing Arts: _____
   Notes: _____

Religious/Cultural Studies:_____
   Notes: _____

Field Trips: _____
   Notes: _____

Trade Skills/Shop:_____
   Notes: _____

Health/Hygiene/Nutrition: _____
   Notes: _____

Computers/Tech./Business Skills: _____
   Notes: _____

Comm. Svc./Volunteerism/Career:_____
   Notes: _____

Home Economics/Chores: _____
   Notes: _____

Electives/Hobbies/Clubs:_____
   Notes: _____

Miscellaneous: _____
_____

Day 35   Date: __ / __ / __   Hours: _____   Admin. Notes: _____

Reading/Literature: _____
  Notes: _____

Writing/Language Arts: _____
  Notes: _____

Mathematics: _____
  Notes: _____

Science/Lab: _____
  Notes: _____

US Hist./Govt./Civics: _____
  Notes: _____

World History/Geography: _____
  Notes: _____

Foreign Language: _____
  Notes: _____

Sports/Fitness/Phys. Ed.: _____
  Notes: _____

Music: _____
  Notes: _____

Visual Arts: _____
  Notes: _____

Performing Arts: _____
  Notes: _____

Religious/Cultural Studies: _____
  Notes: _____

Field Trips: _____
  Notes: _____

Trade Skills/Shop: _____
  Notes: _____

Health/Hygiene/Nutrition: _____
  Notes: _____

Computers/Tech./Business Skills: _____
  Notes: _____

Comm. Svc./Volunteerism/Career: _____
  Notes: _____

Home Economics/Chores: _____
  Notes: _____

Electives/Hobbies/Clubs: _____
  Notes: _____

Miscellaneous: _____

Day 36 Date: __ / __ / __ Hours: _____ Admin. Notes: _____

Reading/Literature: _____
   Notes: _____

Writing/Language Arts: _____
   Notes: _____

Mathematics: _____
   Notes: _____

Science/Lab: _____
   Notes: _____

US Hist./Govt./Civics: _____
   Notes: _____

World History/Geography: _____
   Notes: _____

Foreign Language: _____
   Notes: _____

Sports/Fitness/Phys. Ed.: _____
   Notes: _____

Music: _____
   Notes: _____

Visual Arts: _____
   Notes: _____

Performing Arts: _____
   Notes: _____

Religious/Cultural Studies: _____
   Notes: _____

Field Trips: _____
   Notes: _____

Trade Skills/Shop: _____
   Notes: _____

Health/Hygiene/Nutrition: _____
   Notes: _____

Computers/Tech./Business Skills: _____
   Notes: _____

Comm. Svc./Volunteerism/Career: _____
   Notes: _____

Home Economics/Chores: _____
   Notes: _____

Electives/Hobbies/Clubs: _____
   Notes: _____

Miscellaneous: _____
_____

Day 37 Date: __ /__ /__ Hours: _____ Admin. Notes: _____

Reading/Literature: _____
Notes: _____

Writing/Language Arts: _____
Notes: _____

Mathematics: _____
Notes: _____

Science/Lab: _____
Notes: _____

US Hist./Govt./Civics: _____
Notes: _____

World History/Geography: _____
Notes: _____

Foreign Language: _____
Notes: _____

Sports/Fitness/Phys. Ed.: _____
Notes: _____

Music: _____
Notes: _____

Visual Arts: _____
Notes: _____

Performing Arts: _____
Notes: _____

Religious/Cultural Studies: _____
Notes: _____

Field Trips: _____
Notes: _____

Trade Skills/Shop: _____
Notes: _____

Health/Hygiene/Nutrition: _____
Notes: _____

Computers/Tech./Business Skills: _____
Notes: _____

Comm. Svc./Volunteerism/Career: _____
Notes: _____

Home Economics/Chores: _____
Notes: _____

Electives/Hobbies/Clubs: _____
Notes: _____

Miscellaneous: _____

Day 38 Date: __ /__ /__ Hours: _____ Admin. Notes: _____

Reading/Literature: _____
  Notes: _____

Writing/Language Arts: _____
  Notes: _____

Mathematics: _____
  Notes: _____

Science/Lab: _____
  Notes: _____

US Hist./Govt./Civics: _____
  Notes: _____

World History/Geography: _____
  Notes: _____

Foreign Language: _____
  Notes: _____

Sports/Fitness/Phys. Ed.: _____
  Notes: _____

Music: _____
  Notes: _____

Visual Arts: _____
  Notes: _____

Performing Arts: _____
  Notes: _____

Religious/Cultural Studies: _____
  Notes: _____

Field Trips: _____
  Notes: _____

Trade Skills/Shop: _____
  Notes: _____

Health/Hygiene/Nutrition: _____
  Notes: _____

Computers/Tech./Business Skills: _____
  Notes: _____

Comm. Svc./Volunteerism/Career: _____
  Notes: _____

Home Economics/Chores: _____
  Notes: _____

Electives/Hobbies/Clubs: _____
  Notes: _____

Miscellaneous: _____
_____

Day 39 Date: __ /__ /__ Hours: _____ Admin. Notes:_____

Reading/Literature: _____
  Notes: _____

Writing/Language Arts: _____
  Notes: _____

Mathematics: _____
  Notes: _____

Science/Lab: _____
  Notes: _____

US Hist./Govt./Civics: _____
  Notes: _____

World History/Geography: _____
  Notes: _____

Foreign Language: _____
  Notes: _____

Sports/Fitness/Phys. Ed.: _____
  Notes: _____

Music: _____
  Notes: _____

Visual Arts: _____
  Notes: _____

Performing Arts: _____
  Notes: _____

Religious/Cultural Studies: _____
  Notes: _____

Field Trips: _____
  Notes: _____

Trade Skills/Shop: _____
  Notes: _____

Health/Hygiene/Nutrition: _____
  Notes: _____

Computers/Tech./Business Skills: _____
  Notes: _____

Comm. Svc./Volunteerism/Career: _____
  Notes: _____

Home Economics/Chores: _____
  Notes: _____

Electives/Hobbies/Clubs: _____
  Notes: _____

Miscellaneous: _____

Day 40 Date: __ /__ /__ Hours: _____ Admin. Notes: _____

Reading/Literature: _____
   Notes: _____
Writing/Language Arts: _____
   Notes: _____
Mathematics: _____
   Notes: _____
Science/Lab: _____
   Notes: _____
US Hist./Govt./Civics: _____
   Notes: _____
World History/Geography: _____
   Notes: _____
Foreign Language: _____
   Notes: _____
Sports/Fitness/Phys. Ed.: _____
   Notes: _____
Music: _____
   Notes: _____
Visual Arts: _____
   Notes: _____
Performing Arts: _____
   Notes: _____
Religious/Cultural Studies: _____
   Notes: _____
Field Trips: _____
   Notes: _____
Trade Skills/Shop: _____
   Notes: _____
Health/Hygiene/Nutrition: _____
   Notes: _____
Computers/Tech./Business Skills: _____
   Notes: _____
Comm. Svc./Volunteerism/Career: _____
   Notes: _____
Home Economics/Chores: _____
   Notes: _____
Electives/Hobbies/Clubs: _____
   Notes: _____
Miscellaneous: _____

Day 41 Date: __ /__ /__ Hours: _____ Admin. Notes: _____

Reading/Literature: _____
  Notes: _____

Writing/Language Arts: _____
  Notes: _____

Mathematics: _____
  Notes: _____

Science/Lab: _____
  Notes: _____

US Hist./Govt./Civics: _____
  Notes: _____

World History/Geography: _____
  Notes: _____

Foreign Language: _____
  Notes: _____

Sports/Fitness/Phys. Ed.: _____
  Notes: _____

Music: _____
  Notes: _____

Visual Arts: _____
  Notes: _____

Performing Arts: _____
  Notes: _____

Religious/Cultural Studies: _____
  Notes: _____

Field Trips: _____
  Notes: _____

Trade Skills/Shop: _____
  Notes: _____

Health/Hygiene/Nutrition: _____
  Notes: _____

Computers/Tech./Business Skills: _____
  Notes: _____

Comm. Svc./Volunteerism/Career: _____
  Notes: _____

Home Economics/Chores: _____
  Notes: _____

Electives/Hobbies/Clubs: _____
  Notes: _____

Miscellaneous: _____
_____

Day 42 Date: __ /__ /__ Hours: _____ Admin. Notes: _____

Reading/Literature: _____
   Notes: _____

Writing/Language Arts: _____
   Notes: _____

Mathematics: _____
   Notes: _____

Science/Lab: _____
   Notes: _____

US Hist./Govt./Civics: _____
   Notes: _____

World History/Geography: _____
   Notes: _____

Foreign Language: _____
   Notes: _____

Sports/Fitness/Phys. Ed.: _____
   Notes: _____

Music: _____
   Notes: _____

Visual Arts: _____
   Notes: _____

Performing Arts: _____
   Notes: _____

Religious/Cultural Studies: _____
   Notes: _____

Field Trips: _____
   Notes: _____

Trade Skills/Shop: _____
   Notes: _____

Health/Hygiene/Nutrition: _____
   Notes: _____

Computers/Tech./Business Skills: _____
   Notes: _____

Comm. Svc./Volunteerism/Career: _____
   Notes: _____

Home Economics/Chores: _____
   Notes: _____

Electives/Hobbies/Clubs: _____
   Notes: _____

Miscellaneous: _____
_____

Day 43   Date: __ / __ / __   Hours: _____   Admin. Notes: _____

Reading/Literature: _____
  Notes: _____
Writing/Language Arts: _____
  Notes: _____
Mathematics: _____
  Notes: _____
Science/Lab: _____
  Notes: _____
US Hist./Govt./Civics: _____
  Notes: _____
World History/Geography: _____
  Notes: _____
Foreign Language: _____
  Notes: _____
Sports/Fitness/Phys. Ed.: _____
  Notes: _____
Music: _____
  Notes: _____
Visual Arts: _____
  Notes: _____
Performing Arts: _____
  Notes: _____
Religious/Cultural Studies: _____
  Notes: _____
Field Trips: _____
  Notes: _____
Trade Skills/Shop: _____
  Notes: _____
Health/Hygiene/Nutrition: _____
  Notes: _____
Computers/Tech./Business Skills: _____
  Notes: _____
Comm. Svc./Volunteerism/Career: _____
  Notes: _____
Home Economics/Chores: _____
  Notes: _____
Electives/Hobbies/Clubs: _____
  Notes: _____
Miscellaneous: _____

Day 44 Date: __ /__ /__ Hours: _____ Admin. Notes: _____

Reading/Literature: _____
   Notes: _____

Writing/Language Arts: _____
   Notes: _____

Mathematics: _____
   Notes: _____

Science/Lab: _____
   Notes: _____

US Hist./Govt./Civics: _____
   Notes: _____

World History/Geography: _____
   Notes: _____

Foreign Language: _____
   Notes: _____

Sports/Fitness/Phys. Ed.: _____
   Notes: _____

Music: _____
   Notes: _____

Visual Arts: _____
   Notes: _____

Performing Arts: _____
   Notes: _____

Religious/Cultural Studies: _____
   Notes: _____

Field Trips: _____
   Notes: _____

Trade Skills/Shop: _____
   Notes: _____

Health/Hygiene/Nutrition: _____
   Notes: _____

Computers/Tech./Business Skills: _____
   Notes: _____

Comm. Svc./Volunteerism/Career: _____
   Notes: _____

Home Economics/Chores: _____
   Notes: _____

Electives/Hobbies/Clubs: _____
   Notes: _____

Miscellaneous: _____
_____

Day 45 Date: __ /__ /__ Hours: _____ Admin. Notes: _____

Reading/Literature: _____
Notes: _____
Writing/Language Arts: _____
Notes: _____
Mathematics: _____
Notes: _____
Science/Lab: _____
Notes: _____
US Hist./Govt./Civics: _____
Notes: _____
World History/Geography: _____
Notes: _____
Foreign Language: _____
Notes: _____
Sports/Fitness/Phys. Ed.: _____
Notes: _____
Music: _____
Notes: _____
Visual Arts: _____
Notes: _____
Performing Arts: _____
Notes: _____
Religious/Cultural Studies: _____
Notes: _____
Field Trips: _____
Notes: _____
Trade Skills/Shop: _____
Notes: _____
Health/Hygiene/Nutrition: _____
Notes: _____
Computers/Tech./Business Skills: _____
Notes: _____
Comm. Svc./Volunteerism/Career: _____
Notes: _____
Home Economics/Chores: _____
Notes: _____
Electives/Hobbies/Clubs: _____
Notes: _____
Miscellaneous: _____

Day 46   Date: __ /__ /__   Hours: _____   Admin. Notes: _____

Reading/Literature: _____
  Notes: _____
Writing/Language Arts: _____
  Notes: _____
Mathematics: _____
  Notes: _____
Science/Lab: _____
  Notes: _____
US Hist./Govt./Civics: _____
  Notes: _____
World History/Geography: _____
  Notes: _____
Foreign Language: _____
  Notes: _____
Sports/Fitness/Phys. Ed.: _____
  Notes: _____
Music: _____
  Notes: _____
Visual Arts: _____
  Notes: _____
Performing Arts: _____
  Notes: _____
Religious/Cultural Studies: _____
  Notes: _____
Field Trips: _____
  Notes: _____
Trade Skills/Shop: _____
  Notes: _____
Health/Hygiene/Nutrition: _____
  Notes: _____
Computers/Tech./Business Skills: _____
  Notes: _____
Comm. Svc./Volunteerism/Career: _____
  Notes: _____
Home Economics/Chores: _____
  Notes: _____
Electives/Hobbies/Clubs: _____
  Notes: _____
Miscellaneous: _____

Day 47 Date: __ / __ / __ Hours: _____ Admin. Notes: _____

Reading/Literature: _____
Notes: _____

Writing/Language Arts: _____
Notes: _____

Mathematics: _____
Notes: _____

Science/Lab: _____
Notes: _____

US Hist./Govt./Civics: _____
Notes: _____

World History/Geography: _____
Notes: _____

Foreign Language: _____
Notes: _____

Sports/Fitness/Phys. Ed.: _____
Notes: _____

Music: _____
Notes: _____

Visual Arts: _____
Notes: _____

Performing Arts: _____
Notes: _____

Religious/Cultural Studies: _____
Notes: _____

Field Trips: _____
Notes: _____

Trade Skills/Shop: _____
Notes: _____

Health/Hygiene/Nutrition: _____
Notes: _____

Computers/Tech./Business Skills: _____
Notes: _____

Comm. Svc./Volunteerism/Career: _____
Notes: _____

Home Economics/Chores: _____
Notes: _____

Electives/Hobbies/Clubs: _____
Notes: _____

Miscellaneous: _____

Day 48 Date: __ /__ /__ Hours: _____ Admin. Notes: _____

Reading/Literature: _____
Notes: _____
Writing/Language Arts: _____
Notes: _____
Mathematics: _____
Notes: _____
Science/Lab: _____
Notes: _____
US Hist./Govt./Civics: _____
Notes: _____
World History/Geography: _____
Notes: _____
Foreign Language: _____
Notes: _____
Sports/Fitness/Phys. Ed.: _____
Notes: _____
Music: _____
Notes: _____
Visual Arts: _____
Notes: _____
Performing Arts: _____
Notes: _____
Religious/Cultural Studies: _____
Notes: _____
Field Trips: _____
Notes: _____
Trade Skills/Shop: _____
Notes: _____
Health/Hygiene/Nutrition: _____
Notes: _____
Computers/Tech./Business Skills: _____
Notes: _____
Comm. Svc./Volunteerism/Career: _____
Notes: _____
Home Economics/Chores: _____
Notes: _____
Electives/Hobbies/Clubs: _____
Notes: _____
Miscellaneous: _____
_____

Day 49   Date: __ /__ /__   Hours: _____   Admin. Notes:_____

Reading/Literature: _____
Notes: _____

Writing/Language Arts: _____
Notes: _____

Mathematics: _____
Notes: _____

Science/Lab: _____
Notes: _____

US Hist./Govt./Civics:_____
Notes: _____

World History/Geography: _____
Notes: _____

Foreign Language:_____
Notes: _____

Sports/Fitness/Phys. Ed.: _____
Notes: _____

Music: _____
Notes: _____

Visual Arts:_____
Notes: _____

Performing Arts: _____
Notes: _____

Religious/Cultural Studies: _____
Notes: _____

Field Trips: _____
Notes: _____

Trade Skills/Shop:_____
Notes: _____

Health/Hygiene/Nutrition: _____
Notes: _____

Computers/Tech./Business Skills: _____
Notes: _____

Comm. Svc./Volunteerism/Career:_____
Notes: _____

Home Economics/Chores: _____
Notes: _____

Electives/Hobbies/Clubs:_____
Notes: _____

Miscellaneous: _____
_____

Day 50   Date: __ /__ /__   Hours: _____   Admin. Notes: _____

Reading/Literature: _____
  Notes: _____
Writing/Language Arts: _____
  Notes: _____
Mathematics: _____
  Notes: _____
Science/Lab: _____
  Notes: _____
US Hist./Govt./Civics: _____
  Notes: _____
World History/Geography: _____
  Notes: _____
Foreign Language: _____
  Notes: _____
Sports/Fitness/Phys. Ed.: _____
  Notes: _____
Music: _____
  Notes: _____
Visual Arts: _____
  Notes: _____
Performing Arts: _____
  Notes: _____
Religious/Cultural Studies: _____
  Notes: _____
Field Trips: _____
  Notes: _____
Trade Skills/Shop: _____
  Notes: _____
Health/Hygiene/Nutrition: _____
  Notes: _____
Computers/Tech./Business Skills: _____
  Notes: _____
Comm. Svc./Volunteerism/Career: _____
  Notes: _____
Home Economics/Chores: _____
  Notes: _____
Electives/Hobbies/Clubs: _____
  Notes: _____
Miscellaneous: _____

Day 51 Date: __ / __ / __ Hours: _____ Admin. Notes:_____

Reading/Literature: _____
  Notes: _____
Writing/Language Arts: _____
  Notes: _____
Mathematics: _____
  Notes: _____
Science/Lab: _____
  Notes: _____
US Hist./Govt./Civics: _____
  Notes: _____
World History/Geography: _____
  Notes: _____
Foreign Language: _____
  Notes: _____
Sports/Fitness/Phys. Ed.: _____
  Notes: _____
Music: _____
  Notes: _____
Visual Arts: _____
  Notes: _____
Performing Arts: _____
  Notes: _____
Religious/Cultural Studies: _____
  Notes: _____
Field Trips: _____
  Notes: _____
Trade Skills/Shop: _____
  Notes: _____
Health/Hygiene/Nutrition: _____
  Notes: _____
Computers/Tech./Business Skills: _____
  Notes: _____
Comm. Svc./Volunteerism/Career: _____
  Notes: _____
Home Economics/Chores: _____
  Notes: _____
Electives/Hobbies/Clubs: _____
  Notes: _____
Miscellaneous: _____
_____

Day 52 Date: __ /__ /__ Hours: _____ Admin. Notes: _____

Reading/Literature: _____
   Notes: _____
Writing/Language Arts: _____
   Notes: _____
Mathematics: _____
   Notes: _____
Science/Lab: _____
   Notes: _____
US Hist./Govt./Civics: _____
   Notes: _____
World History/Geography: _____
   Notes: _____
Foreign Language: _____
   Notes: _____
Sports/Fitness/Phys. Ed.: _____
   Notes: _____
Music: _____
   Notes: _____
Visual Arts: _____
   Notes: _____
Performing Arts: _____
   Notes: _____
Religious/Cultural Studies: _____
   Notes: _____
Field Trips: _____
   Notes: _____
Trade Skills/Shop: _____
   Notes: _____
Health/Hygiene/Nutrition: _____
   Notes: _____
Computers/Tech./Business Skills: _____
   Notes: _____
Comm. Svc./Volunteerism/Career: _____
   Notes: _____
Home Economics/Chores: _____
   Notes: _____
Electives/Hobbies/Clubs: _____
   Notes: _____
Miscellaneous: _____
_____

Day 53 Date: __ /__ /__ Hours: _____ Admin. Notes: _____

Reading/Literature: _____
   Notes: _____
Writing/Language Arts: _____
   Notes: _____
Mathematics: _____
   Notes: _____
Science/Lab: _____
   Notes: _____
US Hist./Govt./Civics: _____
   Notes: _____
World History/Geography: _____
   Notes: _____
Foreign Language: _____
   Notes: _____
Sports/Fitness/Phys. Ed.: _____
   Notes: _____
Music: _____
   Notes: _____
Visual Arts: _____
   Notes: _____
Performing Arts: _____
   Notes: _____
Religious/Cultural Studies: _____
   Notes: _____
Field Trips: _____
   Notes: _____
Trade Skills/Shop: _____
   Notes: _____
Health/Hygiene/Nutrition: _____
   Notes: _____
Computers/Tech./Business Skills: _____
   Notes: _____
Comm. Svc./Volunteerism/Career: _____
   Notes: _____
Home Economics/Chores: _____
   Notes: _____
Electives/Hobbies/Clubs: _____
   Notes: _____
Miscellaneous: _____

Day 54 Date: __ /__ /__ Hours: _____ Admin. Notes: _____

Reading/Literature: _____
  Notes: _____
Writing/Language Arts: _____
  Notes: _____
Mathematics: _____
  Notes: _____
Science/Lab: _____
  Notes: _____
US Hist./Govt./Civics: _____
  Notes: _____
World History/Geography: _____
  Notes: _____
Foreign Language: _____
  Notes: _____
Sports/Fitness/Phys. Ed.: _____
  Notes: _____
Music: _____
  Notes: _____
Visual Arts: _____
  Notes: _____
Performing Arts: _____
  Notes: _____
Religious/Cultural Studies: _____
  Notes: _____
Field Trips: _____
  Notes: _____
Trade Skills/Shop: _____
  Notes: _____
Health/Hygiene/Nutrition: _____
  Notes: _____
Computers/Tech./Business Skills: _____
  Notes: _____
Comm. Svc./Volunteerism/Career: _____
  Notes: _____
Home Economics/Chores: _____
  Notes: _____
Electives/Hobbies/Clubs: _____
  Notes: _____
Miscellaneous: _____

Day 55   Date: __ /__ /__   Hours: _____   Admin. Notes:_____

Reading/Literature: _____
  Notes: _____

Writing/Language Arts: _____
  Notes: _____

Mathematics: _____
  Notes: _____

Science/Lab: _____
  Notes: _____

US Hist./Govt./Civics: _____
  Notes: _____

World History/Geography: _____
  Notes: _____

Foreign Language: _____
  Notes: _____

Sports/Fitness/Phys. Ed.: _____
  Notes: _____

Music: _____
  Notes: _____

Visual Arts: _____
  Notes: _____

Performing Arts: _____
  Notes: _____

Religious/Cultural Studies: _____
  Notes: _____

Field Trips: _____
  Notes: _____

Trade Skills/Shop: _____
  Notes: _____

Health/Hygiene/Nutrition: _____
  Notes: _____

Computers/Tech./Business Skills: _____
  Notes: _____

Comm. Svc./Volunteerism/Career: _____
  Notes: _____

Home Economics/Chores: _____
  Notes: _____

Electives/Hobbies/Clubs: _____
  Notes: _____

Miscellaneous: _____

Day 56 Date: __ /__ /__ Hours: _____ Admin. Notes: _____

Reading/Literature: _____
  Notes: _____

Writing/Language Arts: _____
  Notes: _____

Mathematics: _____
  Notes: _____

Science/Lab: _____
  Notes: _____

US Hist./Govt./Civics: _____
  Notes: _____

World History/Geography: _____
  Notes: _____

Foreign Language: _____
  Notes: _____

Sports/Fitness/Phys. Ed.: _____
  Notes: _____

Music: _____
  Notes: _____

Visual Arts: _____
  Notes: _____

Performing Arts: _____
  Notes: _____

Religious/Cultural Studies: _____
  Notes: _____

Field Trips: _____
  Notes: _____

Trade Skills/Shop: _____
  Notes: _____

Health/Hygiene/Nutrition: _____
  Notes: _____

Computers/Tech./Business Skills: _____
  Notes: _____

Comm. Svc./Volunteerism/Career: _____
  Notes: _____

Home Economics/Chores: _____
  Notes: _____

Electives/Hobbies/Clubs: _____
  Notes: _____

Miscellaneous: _____
_____

Day 57 Date: __ /__ /__ Hours: _____ Admin. Notes: _____

Reading/Literature: _____
Notes: _____

Writing/Language Arts: _____
Notes: _____

Mathematics: _____
Notes: _____

Science/Lab: _____
Notes: _____

US Hist./Govt./Civics: _____
Notes: _____

World History/Geography: _____
Notes: _____

Foreign Language: _____
Notes: _____

Sports/Fitness/Phys. Ed.: _____
Notes: _____

Music: _____
Notes: _____

Visual Arts: _____
Notes: _____

Performing Arts: _____
Notes: _____

Religious/Cultural Studies: _____
Notes: _____

Field Trips: _____
Notes: _____

Trade Skills/Shop: _____
Notes: _____

Health/Hygiene/Nutrition: _____
Notes: _____

Computers/Tech./Business Skills: _____
Notes: _____

Comm. Svc./Volunteerism/Career: _____
Notes: _____

Home Economics/Chores: _____
Notes: _____

Electives/Hobbies/Clubs: _____
Notes: _____

Miscellaneous: _____

Day 58   Date: __ /__ /__   Hours: _____   Admin. Notes: _____

Reading/Literature: _____
   Notes: _____
Writing/Language Arts: _____
   Notes: _____
Mathematics: _____
   Notes: _____
Science/Lab: _____
   Notes: _____
US Hist./Govt./Civics: _____
   Notes: _____
World History/Geography: _____
   Notes: _____
Foreign Language: _____
   Notes: _____
Sports/Fitness/Phys. Ed.: _____
   Notes: _____
Music: _____
   Notes: _____
Visual Arts: _____
   Notes: _____
Performing Arts: _____
   Notes: _____
Religious/Cultural Studies: _____
   Notes: _____
Field Trips: _____
   Notes: _____
Trade Skills/Shop: _____
   Notes: _____
Health/Hygiene/Nutrition: _____
   Notes: _____
Computers/Tech./Business Skills: _____
   Notes: _____
Comm. Svc./Volunteerism/Career: _____
   Notes: _____
Home Economics/Chores: _____
   Notes: _____
Electives/Hobbies/Clubs: _____
   Notes: _____
Miscellaneous: _____
_____

Day 59   Date: __ /__ /__   Hours: _____   Admin. Notes:_____

Reading/Literature: _____
  Notes: _____

Writing/Language Arts: _____
  Notes: _____

Mathematics: _____
  Notes: _____

Science/Lab: _____
  Notes: _____

US Hist./Govt./Civics: _____
  Notes: _____

World History/Geography: _____
  Notes: _____

Foreign Language: _____
  Notes: _____

Sports/Fitness/Phys. Ed.: _____
  Notes: _____

Music: _____
  Notes: _____

Visual Arts: _____
  Notes: _____

Performing Arts: _____
  Notes: _____

Religious/Cultural Studies: _____
  Notes: _____

Field Trips: _____
  Notes: _____

Trade Skills/Shop: _____
  Notes: _____

Health/Hygiene/Nutrition: _____
  Notes: _____

Computers/Tech./Business Skills: _____
  Notes: _____

Comm. Svc./Volunteerism/Career: _____
  Notes: _____

Home Economics/Chores: _____
  Notes: _____

Electives/Hobbies/Clubs: _____
  Notes: _____

Miscellaneous: _____

Day 60 Date: __ / __ / __ Hours: _____ Admin. Notes: _____

Reading/Literature: _____
  Notes: _____
Writing/Language Arts: _____
  Notes: _____
Mathematics: _____
  Notes: _____
Science/Lab: _____
  Notes: _____
US Hist./Govt./Civics: _____
  Notes: _____
World History/Geography: _____
  Notes: _____
Foreign Language: _____
  Notes: _____
Sports/Fitness/Phys. Ed.: _____
  Notes: _____
Music: _____
  Notes: _____
Visual Arts: _____
  Notes: _____
Performing Arts: _____
  Notes: _____
Religious/Cultural Studies: _____
  Notes: _____
Field Trips: _____
  Notes: _____
Trade Skills/Shop: _____
  Notes: _____
Health/Hygiene/Nutrition: _____
  Notes: _____
Computers/Tech./Business Skills: _____
  Notes: _____
Comm. Svc./Volunteerism/Career: _____
  Notes: _____
Home Economics/Chores: _____
  Notes: _____
Electives/Hobbies/Clubs: _____
  Notes: _____
Miscellaneous: _____
_____

Day 61   Date: __ / __ / __   Hours: _____   Admin. Notes: _____

Reading/Literature: _____
Notes: _____

Writing/Language Arts: _____
Notes: _____

Mathematics: _____
Notes: _____

Science/Lab: _____
Notes: _____

US Hist./Govt./Civics: _____
Notes: _____

World History/Geography: _____
Notes: _____

Foreign Language: _____
Notes: _____

Sports/Fitness/Phys. Ed.: _____
Notes: _____

Music: _____
Notes: _____

Visual Arts: _____
Notes: _____

Performing Arts: _____
Notes: _____

Religious/Cultural Studies: _____
Notes: _____

Field Trips: _____
Notes: _____

Trade Skills/Shop: _____
Notes: _____

Health/Hygiene/Nutrition: _____
Notes: _____

Computers/Tech./Business Skills: _____
Notes: _____

Comm. Svc./Volunteerism/Career: _____
Notes: _____

Home Economics/Chores: _____
Notes: _____

Electives/Hobbies/Clubs: _____
Notes: _____

Miscellaneous: _____

Day 62   Date: __ / __ / __   Hours: _____   Admin. Notes: _____

Reading/Literature: _____
Notes: _____

Writing/Language Arts: _____
Notes: _____

Mathematics: _____
Notes: _____

Science/Lab: _____
Notes: _____

US Hist./Govt./Civics: _____
Notes: _____

World History/Geography: _____
Notes: _____

Foreign Language: _____
Notes: _____

Sports/Fitness/Phys. Ed.: _____
Notes: _____

Music: _____
Notes: _____

Visual Arts: _____
Notes: _____

Performing Arts: _____
Notes: _____

Religious/Cultural Studies: _____
Notes: _____

Field Trips: _____
Notes: _____

Trade Skills/Shop: _____
Notes: _____

Health/Hygiene/Nutrition: _____
Notes: _____

Computers/Tech./Business Skills: _____
Notes: _____

Comm. Svc./Volunteerism/Career: _____
Notes: _____

Home Economics/Chores: _____
Notes: _____

Electives/Hobbies/Clubs: _____
Notes: _____

Miscellaneous: _____

Day 63   Date: __ /__ /__   Hours: _____   Admin. Notes:_____

Reading/Literature: _____
   Notes: _____

Writing/Language Arts: _____
   Notes: _____

Mathematics: _____
   Notes: _____

Science/Lab: _____
   Notes: _____

US Hist./Govt./Civics: _____
   Notes: _____

World History/Geography: _____
   Notes: _____

Foreign Language: _____
   Notes: _____

Sports/Fitness/Phys. Ed.: _____
   Notes: _____

Music: _____
   Notes: _____

Visual Arts: _____
   Notes: _____

Performing Arts: _____
   Notes: _____

Religious/Cultural Studies: _____
   Notes: _____

Field Trips: _____
   Notes: _____

Trade Skills/Shop: _____
   Notes: _____

Health/Hygiene/Nutrition: _____
   Notes: _____

Computers/Tech./Business Skills: _____
   Notes: _____

Comm. Svc./Volunteerism/Career: _____
   Notes: _____

Home Economics/Chores: _____
   Notes: _____

Electives/Hobbies/Clubs: _____
   Notes: _____

Miscellaneous: _____

Day 64   Date: __ / __ / __   Hours: _____   Admin. Notes: _____

Reading/Literature: _____
  Notes: _____

Writing/Language Arts: _____
  Notes: _____

Mathematics: _____
  Notes: _____

Science/Lab: _____
  Notes: _____

US Hist./Govt./Civics: _____
  Notes: _____

World History/Geography: _____
  Notes: _____

Foreign Language: _____
  Notes: _____

Sports/Fitness/Phys. Ed.: _____
  Notes: _____

Music: _____
  Notes: _____

Visual Arts: _____
  Notes: _____

Performing Arts: _____
  Notes: _____

Religious/Cultural Studies: _____
  Notes: _____

Field Trips: _____
  Notes: _____

Trade Skills/Shop: _____
  Notes: _____

Health/Hygiene/Nutrition: _____
  Notes: _____

Computers/Tech./Business Skills: _____
  Notes: _____

Comm. Svc./Volunteerism/Career: _____
  Notes: _____

Home Economics/Chores: _____
  Notes: _____

Electives/Hobbies/Clubs: _____
  Notes: _____

Miscellaneous: _____
_____

Day 65 Date: __ /__ /__ Hours: _____ Admin. Notes:_____

Reading/Literature: _____
  Notes: _____
Writing/Language Arts: _____
  Notes: _____
Mathematics: _____
  Notes: _____
Science/Lab: _____
  Notes: _____
US Hist./Govt./Civics:_____
  Notes: _____
World History/Geography: _____
  Notes: _____
Foreign Language:_____
  Notes: _____
Sports/Fitness/Phys. Ed.: _____
  Notes: _____
Music: _____
  Notes: _____
Visual Arts:_____
  Notes: _____
Performing Arts: _____
  Notes: _____
Religious/Cultural Studies: _____
  Notes: _____
Field Trips: _____
  Notes: _____
Trade Skills/Shop:_____
  Notes: _____
Health/Hygiene/Nutrition: _____
  Notes: _____
Computers/Tech./Business Skills: _____
  Notes: _____
Comm. Svc./Volunteerism/Career:_____
  Notes: _____
Home Economics/Chores: _____
  Notes: _____
Electives/Hobbies/Clubs:_____
  Notes: _____
Miscellaneous: _____

Day 66 Date: __ /__ /__ Hours: _____ Admin. Notes: _____

Reading/Literature: _____
   Notes: _____
Writing/Language Arts: _____
   Notes: _____
Mathematics: _____
   Notes: _____
Science/Lab: _____
   Notes: _____
US Hist./Govt./Civics: _____
   Notes: _____
World History/Geography: _____
   Notes: _____
Foreign Language: _____
   Notes: _____
Sports/Fitness/Phys. Ed.: _____
   Notes: _____
Music: _____
   Notes: _____
Visual Arts: _____
   Notes: _____
Performing Arts: _____
   Notes: _____
Religious/Cultural Studies: _____
   Notes: _____
Field Trips: _____
   Notes: _____
Trade Skills/Shop: _____
   Notes: _____
Health/Hygiene/Nutrition: _____
   Notes: _____
Computers/Tech./Business Skills: _____
   Notes: _____
Comm. Svc./Volunteerism/Career: _____
   Notes: _____
Home Economics/Chores: _____
   Notes: _____
Electives/Hobbies/Clubs: _____
   Notes: _____
Miscellaneous: _____
_____

Day 67   Date: __ / __ / __   Hours: _____   Admin. Notes: _____

Reading/Literature: _____

Notes: _____

Writing/Language Arts: _____

Notes: _____

Mathematics: _____

Notes: _____

Science/Lab: _____

Notes: _____

US Hist./Govt./Civics: _____

Notes: _____

World History/Geography: _____

Notes: _____

Foreign Language: _____

Notes: _____

Sports/Fitness/Phys. Ed.: _____

Notes: _____

Music: _____

Notes: _____

Visual Arts: _____

Notes: _____

Performing Arts: _____

Notes: _____

Religious/Cultural Studies: _____

Notes: _____

Field Trips: _____

Notes: _____

Trade Skills/Shop: _____

Notes: _____

Health/Hygiene/Nutrition: _____

Notes: _____

Computers/Tech./Business Skills: _____

Notes: _____

Comm. Svc./Volunteerism/Career: _____

Notes: _____

Home Economics/Chores: _____

Notes: _____

Electives/Hobbies/Clubs: _____

Notes: _____

Miscellaneous: _____

_____

Day 68 Date: __ /__ /__ Hours: _____ Admin. Notes: _____

Reading/Literature: _____
   Notes: _____
Writing/Language Arts: _____
   Notes: _____
Mathematics: _____
   Notes: _____
Science/Lab: _____
   Notes: _____
US Hist./Govt./Civics: _____
   Notes: _____
World History/Geography: _____
   Notes: _____
Foreign Language: _____
   Notes: _____
Sports/Fitness/Phys. Ed.: _____
   Notes: _____
Music: _____
   Notes: _____
Visual Arts: _____
   Notes: _____
Performing Arts: _____
   Notes: _____
Religious/Cultural Studies: _____
   Notes: _____
Field Trips: _____
   Notes: _____
Trade Skills/Shop: _____
   Notes: _____
Health/Hygiene/Nutrition: _____
   Notes: _____
Computers/Tech./Business Skills: _____
   Notes: _____
Comm. Svc./Volunteerism/Career: _____
   Notes: _____
Home Economics/Chores: _____
   Notes: _____
Electives/Hobbies/Clubs: _____
   Notes: _____
Miscellaneous: _____
_____

Day 69   Date: __ /__ /__   Hours: _____   Admin. Notes:_____

Reading/Literature: _____
Notes: _____

Writing/Language Arts: _____
Notes: _____

Mathematics: _____
Notes: _____

Science/Lab: _____
Notes: _____

US Hist./Govt./Civics: _____
Notes: _____

World History/Geography: _____
Notes: _____

Foreign Language: _____
Notes: _____

Sports/Fitness/Phys. Ed.: _____
Notes: _____

Music: _____
Notes: _____

Visual Arts: _____
Notes: _____

Performing Arts: _____
Notes: _____

Religious/Cultural Studies: _____
Notes: _____

Field Trips: _____
Notes: _____

Trade Skills/Shop: _____
Notes: _____

Health/Hygiene/Nutrition: _____
Notes: _____

Computers/Tech./Business Skills: _____
Notes: _____

Comm. Svc./Volunteerism/Career: _____
Notes: _____

Home Economics/Chores: _____
Notes: _____

Electives/Hobbies/Clubs: _____
Notes: _____

Miscellaneous: _____

Day 70 Date: __ /__ /__ Hours: _____ Admin. Notes: _____

Reading/Literature: _____
 Notes: _____
Writing/Language Arts: _____
 Notes: _____
Mathematics: _____
 Notes: _____
Science/Lab: _____
 Notes: _____
US Hist./Govt./Civics: _____
 Notes: _____
World History/Geography: _____
 Notes: _____
Foreign Language: _____
 Notes: _____
Sports/Fitness/Phys. Ed.: _____
 Notes: _____
Music: _____
 Notes: _____
Visual Arts: _____
 Notes: _____
Performing Arts: _____
 Notes: _____
Religious/Cultural Studies: _____
 Notes: _____
Field Trips: _____
 Notes: _____
Trade Skills/Shop: _____
 Notes: _____
Health/Hygiene/Nutrition: _____
 Notes: _____
Computers/Tech./Business Skills: _____
 Notes: _____
Comm. Svc./Volunteerism/Career: _____
 Notes: _____
Home Economics/Chores: _____
 Notes: _____
Electives/Hobbies/Clubs: _____
 Notes: _____
Miscellaneous: _____
_____

Day 71 Date: __ /__ /__ Hours: _____ Admin. Notes: _____

Reading/Literature: _____
Notes: _____

Writing/Language Arts: _____
Notes: _____

Mathematics: _____
Notes: _____

Science/Lab: _____
Notes: _____

US Hist./Govt./Civics: _____
Notes: _____

World History/Geography: _____
Notes: _____

Foreign Language: _____
Notes: _____

Sports/Fitness/Phys. Ed.: _____
Notes: _____

Music: _____
Notes: _____

Visual Arts: _____
Notes: _____

Performing Arts: _____
Notes: _____

Religious/Cultural Studies: _____
Notes: _____

Field Trips: _____
Notes: _____

Trade Skills/Shop: _____
Notes: _____

Health/Hygiene/Nutrition: _____
Notes: _____

Computers/Tech./Business Skills: _____
Notes: _____

Comm. Svc./Volunteerism/Career: _____
Notes: _____

Home Economics/Chores: _____
Notes: _____

Electives/Hobbies/Clubs: _____
Notes: _____

Miscellaneous: _____

Day 72 Date: __ /__ /__ Hours: _____ Admin. Notes: _____

Reading/Literature: _____
Notes: _____
Writing/Language Arts: _____
Notes: _____
Mathematics: _____
Notes: _____
Science/Lab: _____
Notes: _____
US Hist./Govt./Civics: _____
Notes: _____
World History/Geography: _____
Notes: _____
Foreign Language: _____
Notes: _____
Sports/Fitness/Phys. Ed.: _____
Notes: _____
Music: _____
Notes: _____
Visual Arts: _____
Notes: _____
Performing Arts: _____
Notes: _____
Religious/Cultural Studies: _____
Notes: _____
Field Trips: _____
Notes: _____
Trade Skills/Shop: _____
Notes: _____
Health/Hygiene/Nutrition: _____
Notes: _____
Computers/Tech./Business Skills: _____
Notes: _____
Comm. Svc./Volunteerism/Career: _____
Notes: _____
Home Economics/Chores: _____
Notes: _____
Electives/Hobbies/Clubs: _____
Notes: _____
Miscellaneous: _____

Day 73 Date: __ /__ /__ Hours: _____ Admin. Notes: _____

Reading/Literature: _____
Notes: _____

Writing/Language Arts: _____
Notes: _____

Mathematics: _____
Notes: _____

Science/Lab: _____
Notes: _____

US Hist./Govt./Civics: _____
Notes: _____

World History/Geography: _____
Notes: _____

Foreign Language: _____
Notes: _____

Sports/Fitness/Phys. Ed.: _____
Notes: _____

Music: _____
Notes: _____

Visual Arts: _____
Notes: _____

Performing Arts: _____
Notes: _____

Religious/Cultural Studies: _____
Notes: _____

Field Trips: _____
Notes: _____

Trade Skills/Shop: _____
Notes: _____

Health/Hygiene/Nutrition: _____
Notes: _____

Computers/Tech./Business Skills: _____
Notes: _____

Comm. Svc./Volunteerism/Career: _____
Notes: _____

Home Economics/Chores: _____
Notes: _____

Electives/Hobbies/Clubs: _____
Notes: _____

Miscellaneous: _____
_____

Day 74 Date: __ /__ /__ Hours: _____ Admin. Notes: _____

Reading/Literature: _____
   Notes: _____

Writing/Language Arts: _____
   Notes: _____

Mathematics: _____
   Notes: _____

Science/Lab: _____
   Notes: _____

US Hist./Govt./Civics: _____
   Notes: _____

World History/Geography: _____
   Notes: _____

Foreign Language: _____
   Notes: _____

Sports/Fitness/Phys. Ed.: _____
   Notes: _____

Music: _____
   Notes: _____

Visual Arts: _____
   Notes: _____

Performing Arts: _____
   Notes: _____

Religious/Cultural Studies: _____
   Notes: _____

Field Trips: _____
   Notes: _____

Trade Skills/Shop: _____
   Notes: _____

Health/Hygiene/Nutrition: _____
   Notes: _____

Computers/Tech./Business Skills: _____
   Notes: _____

Comm. Svc./Volunteerism/Career: _____
   Notes: _____

Home Economics/Chores: _____
   Notes: _____

Electives/Hobbies/Clubs: _____
   Notes: _____

Miscellaneous: _____
_____

Day 75 Date: __ / __ / __ Hours: _____ Admin. Notes: _____

Reading/Literature: _____
  Notes: _____

Writing/Language Arts: _____
  Notes: _____

Mathematics: _____
  Notes: _____

Science/Lab: _____
  Notes: _____

US Hist./Govt./Civics: _____
  Notes: _____

World History/Geography: _____
  Notes: _____

Foreign Language: _____
  Notes: _____

Sports/Fitness/Phys. Ed.: _____
  Notes: _____

Music: _____
  Notes: _____

Visual Arts: _____
  Notes: _____

Performing Arts: _____
  Notes: _____

Religious/Cultural Studies: _____
  Notes: _____

Field Trips: _____
  Notes: _____

Trade Skills/Shop: _____
  Notes: _____

Health/Hygiene/Nutrition: _____
  Notes: _____

Computers/Tech./Business Skills: _____
  Notes: _____

Comm. Svc./Volunteerism/Career: _____
  Notes: _____

Home Economics/Chores: _____
  Notes: _____

Electives/Hobbies/Clubs: _____
  Notes: _____

Miscellaneous: _____

Day 76   Date: __ / __ / __   Hours: _____   Admin. Notes: _____

Reading/Literature: _____
   Notes: _____
Writing/Language Arts: _____
   Notes: _____
Mathematics: _____
   Notes: _____
Science/Lab: _____
   Notes: _____
US Hist./Govt./Civics: _____
   Notes: _____
World History/Geography: _____
   Notes: _____
Foreign Language: _____
   Notes: _____
Sports/Fitness/Phys. Ed.: _____
   Notes: _____
Music: _____
   Notes: _____
Visual Arts: _____
   Notes: _____
Performing Arts: _____
   Notes: _____
Religious/Cultural Studies: _____
   Notes: _____
Field Trips: _____
   Notes: _____
Trade Skills/Shop: _____
   Notes: _____
Health/Hygiene/Nutrition: _____
   Notes: _____
Computers/Tech./Business Skills: _____
   Notes: _____
Comm. Svc./Volunteerism/Career: _____
   Notes: _____
Home Economics/Chores: _____
   Notes: _____
Electives/Hobbies/Clubs: _____
   Notes: _____
Miscellaneous: _____

Day 77   Date: __ /__ /__   Hours: _____   Admin. Notes: _____

Reading/Literature: _____
Notes: _____

Writing/Language Arts: _____
Notes: _____

Mathematics: _____
Notes: _____

Science/Lab: _____
Notes: _____

US Hist./Govt./Civics: _____
Notes: _____

World History/Geography: _____
Notes: _____

Foreign Language: _____
Notes: _____

Sports/Fitness/Phys. Ed.: _____
Notes: _____

Music: _____
Notes: _____

Visual Arts: _____
Notes: _____

Performing Arts: _____
Notes: _____

Religious/Cultural Studies: _____
Notes: _____

Field Trips: _____
Notes: _____

Trade Skills/Shop: _____
Notes: _____

Health/Hygiene/Nutrition: _____
Notes: _____

Computers/Tech./Business Skills: _____
Notes: _____

Comm. Svc./Volunteerism/Career: _____
Notes: _____

Home Economics/Chores: _____
Notes: _____

Electives/Hobbies/Clubs: _____
Notes: _____

Miscellaneous: _____

Day 78 Date: __ /__ /__ Hours: _____ Admin. Notes: _____

Reading/Literature: _____
   Notes: _____
Writing/Language Arts: _____
   Notes: _____
Mathematics: _____
   Notes: _____
Science/Lab: _____
   Notes: _____
US Hist./Govt./Civics: _____
   Notes: _____
World History/Geography: _____
   Notes: _____
Foreign Language: _____
   Notes: _____
Sports/Fitness/Phys. Ed.: _____
   Notes: _____
Music: _____
   Notes: _____
Visual Arts: _____
   Notes: _____
Performing Arts: _____
   Notes: _____
Religious/Cultural Studies: _____
   Notes: _____
Field Trips: _____
   Notes: _____
Trade Skills/Shop: _____
   Notes: _____
Health/Hygiene/Nutrition: _____
   Notes: _____
Computers/Tech./Business Skills: _____
   Notes: _____
Comm. Svc./Volunteerism/Career: _____
   Notes: _____
Home Economics/Chores: _____
   Notes: _____
Electives/Hobbies/Clubs: _____
   Notes: _____
Miscellaneous: _____

Day 79 Date: __ /__ /__ Hours: _____ Admin. Notes: _____

Reading/Literature: _____
  Notes: _____

Writing/Language Arts: _____
  Notes: _____

Mathematics: _____
  Notes: _____

Science/Lab: _____
  Notes: _____

US Hist./Govt./Civics: _____
  Notes: _____

World History/Geography: _____
  Notes: _____

Foreign Language: _____
  Notes: _____

Sports/Fitness/Phys. Ed.: _____
  Notes: _____

Music: _____
  Notes: _____

Visual Arts: _____
  Notes: _____

Performing Arts: _____
  Notes: _____

Religious/Cultural Studies: _____
  Notes: _____

Field Trips: _____
  Notes: _____

Trade Skills/Shop: _____
  Notes: _____

Health/Hygiene/Nutrition: _____
  Notes: _____

Computers/Tech./Business Skills: _____
  Notes: _____

Comm. Svc./Volunteerism/Career: _____
  Notes: _____

Home Economics/Chores: _____
  Notes: _____

Electives/Hobbies/Clubs: _____
  Notes: _____

Miscellaneous: _____
_____

Day 80 Date: __ /__ /__ Hours: _____ Admin. Notes: _____

Reading/Literature: _____
Notes: _____

Writing/Language Arts: _____
Notes: _____

Mathematics: _____
Notes: _____

Science/Lab: _____
Notes: _____

US Hist./Govt./Civics: _____
Notes: _____

World History/Geography: _____
Notes: _____

Foreign Language: _____
Notes: _____

Sports/Fitness/Phys. Ed.: _____
Notes: _____

Music: _____
Notes: _____

Visual Arts: _____
Notes: _____

Performing Arts: _____
Notes: _____

Religious/Cultural Studies: _____
Notes: _____

Field Trips: _____
Notes: _____

Trade Skills/Shop: _____
Notes: _____

Health/Hygiene/Nutrition: _____
Notes: _____

Computers/Tech./Business Skills: _____
Notes: _____

Comm. Svc./Volunteerism/Career: _____
Notes: _____

Home Economics/Chores: _____
Notes: _____

Electives/Hobbies/Clubs: _____
Notes: _____

Miscellaneous: _____

Day 81 Date: __ /__ /__ Hours: _____ Admin. Notes: _____

Reading/Literature: _____
Notes: _____

Writing/Language Arts: _____
Notes: _____

Mathematics: _____
Notes: _____

Science/Lab: _____
Notes: _____

US Hist./Govt./Civics: _____
Notes: _____

World History/Geography: _____
Notes: _____

Foreign Language: _____
Notes: _____

Sports/Fitness/Phys. Ed.: _____
Notes: _____

Music: _____
Notes: _____

Visual Arts: _____
Notes: _____

Performing Arts: _____
Notes: _____

Religious/Cultural Studies: _____
Notes: _____

Field Trips: _____
Notes: _____

Trade Skills/Shop: _____
Notes: _____

Health/Hygiene/Nutrition: _____
Notes: _____

Computers/Tech./Business Skills: _____
Notes: _____

Comm. Svc./Volunteerism/Career: _____
Notes: _____

Home Economics/Chores: _____
Notes: _____

Electives/Hobbies/Clubs: _____
Notes: _____

Miscellaneous: _____

Day 82   Date: __ /__ /__   Hours: _____   Admin. Notes: _____

Reading/Literature: _____
  Notes: _____
Writing/Language Arts: _____
  Notes: _____
Mathematics: _____
  Notes: _____
Science/Lab: _____
  Notes: _____
US Hist./Govt./Civics: _____
  Notes: _____
World History/Geography: _____
  Notes: _____
Foreign Language: _____
  Notes: _____
Sports/Fitness/Phys. Ed.: _____
  Notes: _____
Music: _____
  Notes: _____
Visual Arts: _____
  Notes: _____
Performing Arts: _____
  Notes: _____
Religious/Cultural Studies: _____
  Notes: _____
Field Trips: _____
  Notes: _____
Trade Skills/Shop: _____
  Notes: _____
Health/Hygiene/Nutrition: _____
  Notes: _____
Computers/Tech./Business Skills: _____
  Notes: _____
Comm. Svc./Volunteerism/Career: _____
  Notes: _____
Home Economics/Chores: _____
  Notes: _____
Electives/Hobbies/Clubs: _____
  Notes: _____
Miscellaneous: _____

Day 83 Date: __ /__ /__ Hours: _____ Admin. Notes:_____

Reading/Literature: _____
  Notes: _____
Writing/Language Arts: _____
  Notes: _____
Mathematics: _____
  Notes: _____
Science/Lab: _____
  Notes: _____
US Hist./Govt./Civics: _____
  Notes: _____
World History/Geography: _____
  Notes: _____
Foreign Language: _____
  Notes: _____
Sports/Fitness/Phys. Ed.: _____
  Notes: _____
Music: _____
  Notes: _____
Visual Arts: _____
  Notes: _____
Performing Arts: _____
  Notes: _____
Religious/Cultural Studies: _____
  Notes: _____
Field Trips: _____
  Notes: _____
Trade Skills/Shop: _____
  Notes: _____
Health/Hygiene/Nutrition: _____
  Notes: _____
Computers/Tech./Business Skills: _____
  Notes: _____
Comm. Svc./Volunteerism/Career: _____
  Notes: _____
Home Economics/Chores: _____
  Notes: _____
Electives/Hobbies/Clubs: _____
  Notes: _____
Miscellaneous: _____
_____

Day 84   Date: __ /__ /__   Hours: _____   Admin. Notes: _____

Reading/Literature: _____
  Notes: _____

Writing/Language Arts: _____
  Notes: _____

Mathematics: _____
  Notes: _____

Science/Lab: _____
  Notes: _____

US Hist./Govt./Civics: _____
  Notes: _____

World History/Geography: _____
  Notes: _____

Foreign Language: _____
  Notes: _____

Sports/Fitness/Phys. Ed.: _____
  Notes: _____

Music: _____
  Notes: _____

Visual Arts: _____
  Notes: _____

Performing Arts: _____
  Notes: _____

Religious/Cultural Studies: _____
  Notes: _____

Field Trips: _____
  Notes: _____

Trade Skills/Shop: _____
  Notes: _____

Health/Hygiene/Nutrition: _____
  Notes: _____

Computers/Tech./Business Skills: _____
  Notes: _____

Comm. Svc./Volunteerism/Career: _____
  Notes: _____

Home Economics/Chores: _____
  Notes: _____

Electives/Hobbies/Clubs: _____
  Notes: _____

Miscellaneous: _____
_____

Day 85 Date: __ /__ /__ Hours: _____ Admin. Notes: _____

Reading/Literature: _____
Notes: _____

Writing/Language Arts: _____
Notes: _____

Mathematics: _____
Notes: _____

Science/Lab: _____
Notes: _____

US Hist./Govt./Civics: _____
Notes: _____

World History/Geography: _____
Notes: _____

Foreign Language: _____
Notes: _____

Sports/Fitness/Phys. Ed.: _____
Notes: _____

Music: _____
Notes: _____

Visual Arts: _____
Notes: _____

Performing Arts: _____
Notes: _____

Religious/Cultural Studies: _____
Notes: _____

Field Trips: _____
Notes: _____

Trade Skills/Shop: _____
Notes: _____

Health/Hygiene/Nutrition: _____
Notes: _____

Computers/Tech./Business Skills: _____
Notes: _____

Comm. Svc./Volunteerism/Career: _____
Notes: _____

Home Economics/Chores: _____
Notes: _____

Electives/Hobbies/Clubs: _____
Notes: _____

Miscellaneous: _____

Day 86 Date: __ /__ /__ Hours: _____ Admin. Notes: _____

Reading/Literature: _____
  Notes: _____
Writing/Language Arts: _____
  Notes: _____
Mathematics: _____
  Notes: _____
Science/Lab: _____
  Notes: _____
US Hist./Govt./Civics: _____
  Notes: _____
World History/Geography: _____
  Notes: _____
Foreign Language: _____
  Notes: _____
Sports/Fitness/Phys. Ed.: _____
  Notes: _____
Music: _____
  Notes: _____
Visual Arts: _____
  Notes: _____
Performing Arts: _____
  Notes: _____
Religious/Cultural Studies: _____
  Notes: _____
Field Trips: _____
  Notes: _____
Trade Skills/Shop: _____
  Notes: _____
Health/Hygiene/Nutrition: _____
  Notes: _____
Computers/Tech./Business Skills: _____
  Notes: _____
Comm. Svc./Volunteerism/Career: _____
  Notes: _____
Home Economics/Chores: _____
  Notes: _____
Electives/Hobbies/Clubs: _____
  Notes: _____
Miscellaneous: _____
_____

Day 87 Date: __ / __ / __ Hours: _____ Admin. Notes: _____

Reading/Literature: _____
  Notes: _____
Writing/Language Arts: _____
  Notes: _____
Mathematics: _____
  Notes: _____
Science/Lab: _____
  Notes: _____
US Hist./Govt./Civics: _____
  Notes: _____
World History/Geography: _____
  Notes: _____
Foreign Language: _____
  Notes: _____
Sports/Fitness/Phys. Ed.: _____
  Notes: _____
Music: _____
  Notes: _____
Visual Arts: _____
  Notes: _____
Performing Arts: _____
  Notes: _____
Religious/Cultural Studies: _____
  Notes: _____
Field Trips: _____
  Notes: _____
Trade Skills/Shop: _____
  Notes: _____
Health/Hygiene/Nutrition: _____
  Notes: _____
Computers/Tech./Business Skills: _____
  Notes: _____
Comm. Svc./Volunteerism/Career: _____
  Notes: _____
Home Economics/Chores: _____
  Notes: _____
Electives/Hobbies/Clubs: _____
  Notes: _____
Miscellaneous: _____

Day 88 Date: __ /__ /__ Hours: _____ Admin. Notes: _____

Reading/Literature: _____
  Notes: _____

Writing/Language Arts: _____
  Notes: _____

Mathematics: _____
  Notes: _____

Science/Lab: _____
  Notes: _____

US Hist./Govt./Civics: _____
  Notes: _____

World History/Geography: _____
  Notes: _____

Foreign Language: _____
  Notes: _____

Sports/Fitness/Phys. Ed.: _____
  Notes: _____

Music: _____
  Notes: _____

Visual Arts: _____
  Notes: _____

Performing Arts: _____
  Notes: _____

Religious/Cultural Studies: _____
  Notes: _____

Field Trips: _____
  Notes: _____

Trade Skills/Shop: _____
  Notes: _____

Health/Hygiene/Nutrition: _____
  Notes: _____

Computers/Tech./Business Skills: _____
  Notes: _____

Comm. Svc./Volunteerism/Career: _____
  Notes: _____

Home Economics/Chores: _____
  Notes: _____

Electives/Hobbies/Clubs: _____
  Notes: _____

Miscellaneous: _____

Day 89 Date: __ /__ /__ Hours: _____ Admin. Notes:_____

Reading/Literature: _____
Notes: _____

Writing/Language Arts: _____
Notes: _____

Mathematics: _____
Notes: _____

Science/Lab: _____
Notes: _____

US Hist./Govt./Civics:_____
Notes: _____

World History/Geography: _____
Notes: _____

Foreign Language:_____
Notes: _____

Sports/Fitness/Phys. Ed.: _____
Notes: _____

Music: _____
Notes: _____

Visual Arts:_____
Notes: _____

Performing Arts: _____
Notes: _____

Religious/Cultural Studies: _____
Notes: _____

Field Trips: _____
Notes: _____

Trade Skills/Shop:_____
Notes: _____

Health/Hygiene/Nutrition: _____
Notes: _____

Computers/Tech./Business Skills: _____
Notes: _____

Comm. Svc./Volunteerism/Career:_____
Notes: _____

Home Economics/Chores: _____
Notes: _____

Electives/Hobbies/Clubs:_____
Notes: _____

Miscellaneous: _____
_____

Day 90 Date: __ /__ /__ Hours: _____ Admin. Notes: _____

Reading/Literature: _____
   Notes: _____
Writing/Language Arts: _____
   Notes: _____
Mathematics: _____
   Notes: _____
Science/Lab: _____
   Notes: _____
US Hist./Govt./Civics: _____
   Notes: _____
World History/Geography: _____
   Notes: _____
Foreign Language: _____
   Notes: _____
Sports/Fitness/Phys. Ed.: _____
   Notes: _____
Music: _____
   Notes: _____
Visual Arts: _____
   Notes: _____
Performing Arts: _____
   Notes: _____
Religious/Cultural Studies: _____
   Notes: _____
Field Trips: _____
   Notes: _____
Trade Skills/Shop: _____
   Notes: _____
Health/Hygiene/Nutrition: _____
   Notes: _____
Computers/Tech./Business Skills: _____
   Notes: _____
Comm. Svc./Volunteerism/Career: _____
   Notes: _____
Home Economics/Chores: _____
   Notes: _____
Electives/Hobbies/Clubs: _____
   Notes: _____
Miscellaneous: _____

Day 91 Date: __ /__ /__ Hours: _____ Admin. Notes: _____

Reading/Literature: _____
Notes: _____

Writing/Language Arts: _____
Notes: _____

Mathematics: _____
Notes: _____

Science/Lab: _____
Notes: _____

US Hist./Govt./Civics: _____
Notes: _____

World History/Geography: _____
Notes: _____

Foreign Language: _____
Notes: _____

Sports/Fitness/Phys. Ed.: _____
Notes: _____

Music: _____
Notes: _____

Visual Arts: _____
Notes: _____

Performing Arts: _____
Notes: _____

Religious/Cultural Studies: _____
Notes: _____

Field Trips: _____
Notes: _____

Trade Skills/Shop: _____
Notes: _____

Health/Hygiene/Nutrition: _____
Notes: _____

Computers/Tech./Business Skills: _____
Notes: _____

Comm. Svc./Volunteerism/Career: _____
Notes: _____

Home Economics/Chores: _____
Notes: _____

Electives/Hobbies/Clubs: _____
Notes: _____

Miscellaneous: _____
_____

Day 92 Date: __ /__ /__ Hours: _____ Admin. Notes: _____

Reading/Literature: _____
 Notes: _____

Writing/Language Arts: _____
 Notes: _____

Mathematics: _____
 Notes: _____

Science/Lab: _____
 Notes: _____

US Hist./Govt./Civics: _____
 Notes: _____

World History/Geography: _____
 Notes: _____

Foreign Language: _____
 Notes: _____

Sports/Fitness/Phys. Ed.: _____
 Notes: _____

Music: _____
 Notes: _____

Visual Arts: _____
 Notes: _____

Performing Arts: _____
 Notes: _____

Religious/Cultural Studies: _____
 Notes: _____

Field Trips: _____
 Notes: _____

Trade Skills/Shop: _____
 Notes: _____

Health/Hygiene/Nutrition: _____
 Notes: _____

Computers/Tech./Business Skills: _____
 Notes: _____

Comm. Svc./Volunteerism/Career: _____
 Notes: _____

Home Economics/Chores: _____
 Notes: _____

Electives/Hobbies/Clubs: _____
 Notes: _____

Miscellaneous: _____
_____

Day 93   Date: __ /__ /__   Hours: _____   Admin. Notes: _____

Reading/Literature: _____
Notes: _____

Writing/Language Arts: _____
Notes: _____

Mathematics: _____
Notes: _____

Science/Lab: _____
Notes: _____

US Hist./Govt./Civics: _____
Notes: _____

World History/Geography: _____
Notes: _____

Foreign Language: _____
Notes: _____

Sports/Fitness/Phys. Ed.: _____
Notes: _____

Music: _____
Notes: _____

Visual Arts: _____
Notes: _____

Performing Arts: _____
Notes: _____

Religious/Cultural Studies: _____
Notes: _____

Field Trips: _____
Notes: _____

Trade Skills/Shop: _____
Notes: _____

Health/Hygiene/Nutrition: _____
Notes: _____

Computers/Tech./Business Skills: _____
Notes: _____

Comm. Svc./Volunteerism/Career: _____
Notes: _____

Home Economics/Chores: _____
Notes: _____

Electives/Hobbies/Clubs: _____
Notes: _____

Miscellaneous: _____

Day 94   Date: __ /__ /__   Hours: _____   Admin. Notes: _____

Reading/Literature: _____
   Notes: _____
Writing/Language Arts: _____
   Notes: _____
Mathematics: _____
   Notes: _____
Science/Lab: _____
   Notes: _____
US Hist./Govt./Civics: _____
   Notes: _____
World History/Geography: _____
   Notes: _____
Foreign Language: _____
   Notes: _____
Sports/Fitness/Phys. Ed.: _____
   Notes: _____
Music: _____
   Notes: _____
Visual Arts: _____
   Notes: _____
Performing Arts: _____
   Notes: _____
Religious/Cultural Studies: _____
   Notes: _____
Field Trips: _____
   Notes: _____
Trade Skills/Shop: _____
   Notes: _____
Health/Hygiene/Nutrition: _____
   Notes: _____
Computers/Tech./Business Skills: _____
   Notes: _____
Comm. Svc./Volunteerism/Career: _____
   Notes: _____
Home Economics/Chores: _____
   Notes: _____
Electives/Hobbies/Clubs: _____
   Notes: _____
Miscellaneous: _____
_____

Day 95   Date: __ /__ /__   Hours: _____   Admin. Notes:_____

Reading/Literature: _____
   Notes: _____
Writing/Language Arts: _____
   Notes: _____
Mathematics: _____
   Notes: _____
Science/Lab: _____
   Notes: _____
US Hist./Govt./Civics:_____
   Notes: _____
World History/Geography: _____
   Notes: _____
Foreign Language: _____
   Notes: _____
Sports/Fitness/Phys. Ed.: _____
   Notes: _____
Music: _____
   Notes: _____
Visual Arts:_____
   Notes: _____
Performing Arts: _____
   Notes: _____
Religious/Cultural Studies: _____
   Notes: _____
Field Trips: _____
   Notes: _____
Trade Skills/Shop:_____
   Notes: _____
Health/Hygiene/Nutrition: _____
   Notes: _____
Computers/Tech./Business Skills: _____
   Notes: _____
Comm. Svc./Volunteerism/Career:_____
   Notes: _____
Home Economics/Chores: _____
   Notes: _____
Electives/Hobbies/Clubs:_____
   Notes: _____
Miscellaneous: _____
_____

Day 96 Date: __ /__ /__ Hours: _____ Admin. Notes: _____

Reading/Literature: _____
   Notes: _____
Writing/Language Arts: _____
   Notes: _____
Mathematics: _____
   Notes: _____
Science/Lab: _____
   Notes: _____
US Hist./Govt./Civics: _____
   Notes: _____
World History/Geography: _____
   Notes: _____
Foreign Language: _____
   Notes: _____
Sports/Fitness/Phys. Ed.: _____
   Notes: _____
Music: _____
   Notes: _____
Visual Arts: _____
   Notes: _____
Performing Arts: _____
   Notes: _____
Religious/Cultural Studies: _____
   Notes: _____
Field Trips: _____
   Notes: _____
Trade Skills/Shop: _____
   Notes: _____
Health/Hygiene/Nutrition: _____
   Notes: _____
Computers/Tech./Business Skills: _____
   Notes: _____
Comm. Svc./Volunteerism/Career: _____
   Notes: _____
Home Economics/Chores: _____
   Notes: _____
Electives/Hobbies/Clubs: _____
   Notes: _____
Miscellaneous: _____

Day 97   Date: __ /__ /__   Hours: _____   Admin. Notes: _____

Reading/Literature: _____
Notes: _____

Writing/Language Arts: _____
Notes: _____

Mathematics: _____
Notes: _____

Science/Lab: _____
Notes: _____

US Hist./Govt./Civics: _____
Notes: _____

World History/Geography: _____
Notes: _____

Foreign Language: _____
Notes: _____

Sports/Fitness/Phys. Ed.: _____
Notes: _____

Music: _____
Notes: _____

Visual Arts: _____
Notes: _____

Performing Arts: _____
Notes: _____

Religious/Cultural Studies: _____
Notes: _____

Field Trips: _____
Notes: _____

Trade Skills/Shop: _____
Notes: _____

Health/Hygiene/Nutrition: _____
Notes: _____

Computers/Tech./Business Skills: _____
Notes: _____

Comm. Svc./Volunteerism/Career: _____
Notes: _____

Home Economics/Chores: _____
Notes: _____

Electives/Hobbies/Clubs: _____
Notes: _____

Miscellaneous: _____

Day 98 Date: __ /__ /__ Hours: _____ Admin. Notes: _____

Reading/Literature: _____
Notes: _____

Writing/Language Arts: _____
Notes: _____

Mathematics: _____
Notes: _____

Science/Lab: _____
Notes: _____

US Hist./Govt./Civics: _____
Notes: _____

World History/Geography: _____
Notes: _____

Foreign Language: _____
Notes: _____

Sports/Fitness/Phys. Ed.: _____
Notes: _____

Music: _____
Notes: _____

Visual Arts: _____
Notes: _____

Performing Arts: _____
Notes: _____

Religious/Cultural Studies: _____
Notes: _____

Field Trips: _____
Notes: _____

Trade Skills/Shop: _____
Notes: _____

Health/Hygiene/Nutrition: _____
Notes: _____

Computers/Tech./Business Skills: _____
Notes: _____

Comm. Svc./Volunteerism/Career: _____
Notes: _____

Home Economics/Chores: _____
Notes: _____

Electives/Hobbies/Clubs: _____
Notes: _____

Miscellaneous: _____
_____

Day 99 Date: __ /__ /__ Hours: _____ Admin. Notes:_____

Reading/Literature: _____
  Notes: _____
Writing/Language Arts: _____
  Notes: _____
Mathematics: _____
  Notes: _____
Science/Lab: _____
  Notes: _____
US Hist./Govt./Civics: _____
  Notes: _____
World History/Geography: _____
  Notes: _____
Foreign Language: _____
  Notes: _____
Sports/Fitness/Phys. Ed.: _____
  Notes: _____
Music: _____
  Notes: _____
Visual Arts: _____
  Notes: _____
Performing Arts: _____
  Notes: _____
Religious/Cultural Studies: _____
  Notes: _____
Field Trips: _____
  Notes: _____
Trade Skills/Shop: _____
  Notes: _____
Health/Hygiene/Nutrition: _____
  Notes: _____
Computers/Tech./Business Skills: _____
  Notes: _____
Comm. Svc./Volunteerism/Career: _____
  Notes: _____
Home Economics/Chores: _____
  Notes: _____
Electives/Hobbies/Clubs: _____
  Notes: _____
Miscellaneous: _____

Day 100 Date: __ /__ /__ Hours: _____ Admin. Notes: _____

Reading/Literature: _____

Notes: _____

Writing/Language Arts: _____

Notes: _____

Mathematics: _____

Notes: _____

Science/Lab: _____

Notes: _____

US Hist./Govt./Civics: _____

Notes: _____

World History/Geography: _____

Notes: _____

Foreign Language: _____

Notes: _____

Sports/Fitness/Phys. Ed.: _____

Notes: _____

Music: _____

Notes: _____

Visual Arts: _____

Notes: _____

Performing Arts: _____

Notes: _____

Religious/Cultural Studies: _____

Notes: _____

Field Trips: _____

Notes: _____

Trade Skills/Shop: _____

Notes: _____

Health/Hygiene/Nutrition: _____

Notes: _____

Computers/Tech./Business Skills: _____

Notes: _____

Comm. Svc./Volunteerism/Career: _____

Notes: _____

Home Economics/Chores: _____

Notes: _____

Electives/Hobbies/Clubs: _____

Notes: _____

Miscellaneous: _____

_____

Day 101 Date: __ /__ /__ Hours: _____ Admin. Notes:_____

Reading/Literature: _____
  Notes: _____
Writing/Language Arts: _____
  Notes: _____
Mathematics: _____
  Notes: _____
Science/Lab: _____
  Notes: _____
US Hist./Govt./Civics: _____
  Notes: _____
World History/Geography: _____
  Notes: _____
Foreign Language: _____
  Notes: _____
Sports/Fitness/Phys. Ed.: _____
  Notes: _____
Music: _____
  Notes: _____
Visual Arts: _____
  Notes: _____
Performing Arts: _____
  Notes: _____
Religious/Cultural Studies: _____
  Notes: _____
Field Trips: _____
  Notes: _____
Trade Skills/Shop: _____
  Notes: _____
Health/Hygiene/Nutrition: _____
  Notes: _____
Computers/Tech./Business Skills: _____
  Notes: _____
Comm. Svc./Volunteerism/Career: _____
  Notes: _____
Home Economics/Chores: _____
  Notes: _____
Electives/Hobbies/Clubs: _____
  Notes: _____
Miscellaneous: _____

Day 102   Date: __ /__ /__   Hours: _____   Admin. Notes: _____

Reading/Literature: _____
   Notes: _____

Writing/Language Arts: _____
   Notes: _____

Mathematics: _____
   Notes: _____

Science/Lab: _____
   Notes: _____

US Hist./Govt./Civics: _____
   Notes: _____

World History/Geography: _____
   Notes: _____

Foreign Language: _____
   Notes: _____

Sports/Fitness/Phys. Ed.: _____
   Notes: _____

Music: _____
   Notes: _____

Visual Arts: _____
   Notes: _____

Performing Arts: _____
   Notes: _____

Religious/Cultural Studies: _____
   Notes: _____

Field Trips: _____
   Notes: _____

Trade Skills/Shop: _____
   Notes: _____

Health/Hygiene/Nutrition: _____
   Notes: _____

Computers/Tech./Business Skills: _____
   Notes: _____

Comm. Svc./Volunteerism/Career: _____
   Notes: _____

Home Economics/Chores: _____
   Notes: _____

Electives/Hobbies/Clubs: _____
   Notes: _____

Miscellaneous: _____
_____

Day 103   Date: __ /__ /__   Hours: _____   Admin. Notes: _____

Reading/Literature: _____
  Notes: _____
Writing/Language Arts: _____
  Notes: _____
Mathematics: _____
  Notes: _____
Science/Lab: _____
  Notes: _____
US Hist./Govt./Civics: _____
  Notes: _____
World History/Geography: _____
  Notes: _____
Foreign Language: _____
  Notes: _____
Sports/Fitness/Phys. Ed.: _____
  Notes: _____
Music: _____
  Notes: _____
Visual Arts: _____
  Notes: _____
Performing Arts: _____
  Notes: _____
Religious/Cultural Studies: _____
  Notes: _____
Field Trips: _____
  Notes: _____
Trade Skills/Shop: _____
  Notes: _____
Health/Hygiene/Nutrition: _____
  Notes: _____
Computers/Tech./Business Skills: _____
  Notes: _____
Comm. Svc./Volunteerism/Career: _____
  Notes: _____
Home Economics/Chores: _____
  Notes: _____
Electives/Hobbies/Clubs: _____
  Notes: _____
Miscellaneous: _____
_____

Day 104 Date: __ /__ /__ Hours: _____ Admin. Notes: _____

Reading/Literature: _____
Notes: _____

Writing/Language Arts: _____
Notes: _____

Mathematics: _____
Notes: _____

Science/Lab: _____
Notes: _____

US Hist./Govt./Civics: _____
Notes: _____

World History/Geography: _____
Notes: _____

Foreign Language: _____
Notes: _____

Sports/Fitness/Phys. Ed.: _____
Notes: _____

Music: _____
Notes: _____

Visual Arts: _____
Notes: _____

Performing Arts: _____
Notes: _____

Religious/Cultural Studies: _____
Notes: _____

Field Trips: _____
Notes: _____

Trade Skills/Shop: _____
Notes: _____

Health/Hygiene/Nutrition: _____
Notes: _____

Computers/Tech./Business Skills: _____
Notes: _____

Comm. Svc./Volunteerism/Career: _____
Notes: _____

Home Economics/Chores: _____
Notes: _____

Electives/Hobbies/Clubs: _____
Notes: _____

Miscellaneous: _____

Day 105   Date: __ /__ /__   Hours: _____   Admin. Notes: _____

Reading/Literature: _____
Notes: _____
Writing/Language Arts: _____
Notes: _____
Mathematics: _____
Notes: _____
Science/Lab: _____
Notes: _____
US Hist./Govt./Civics: _____
Notes: _____
World History/Geography: _____
Notes: _____
Foreign Language: _____
Notes: _____
Sports/Fitness/Phys. Ed.: _____
Notes: _____
Music: _____
Notes: _____
Visual Arts: _____
Notes: _____
Performing Arts: _____
Notes: _____
Religious/Cultural Studies: _____
Notes: _____
Field Trips: _____
Notes: _____
Trade Skills/Shop: _____
Notes: _____
Health/Hygiene/Nutrition: _____
Notes: _____
Computers/Tech./Business Skills: _____
Notes: _____
Comm. Svc./Volunteerism/Career: _____
Notes: _____
Home Economics/Chores: _____
Notes: _____
Electives/Hobbies/Clubs: _____
Notes: _____
Miscellaneous: _____
_____

Day 106   Date: __ /__ /__   Hours: _____   Admin. Notes: _____

Reading/Literature: _____
    Notes: _____

Writing/Language Arts: _____
    Notes: _____

Mathematics: _____
    Notes: _____

Science/Lab: _____
    Notes: _____

US Hist./Govt./Civics: _____
    Notes: _____

World History/Geography: _____
    Notes: _____

Foreign Language: _____
    Notes: _____

Sports/Fitness/Phys. Ed.: _____
    Notes: _____

Music: _____
    Notes: _____

Visual Arts: _____
    Notes: _____

Performing Arts: _____
    Notes: _____

Religious/Cultural Studies: _____
    Notes: _____

Field Trips: _____
    Notes: _____

Trade Skills/Shop: _____
    Notes: _____

Health/Hygiene/Nutrition: _____
    Notes: _____

Computers/Tech./Business Skills: _____
    Notes: _____

Comm. Svc./Volunteerism/Career: _____
    Notes: _____

Home Economics/Chores: _____
    Notes: _____

Electives/Hobbies/Clubs: _____
    Notes: _____

Miscellaneous: _____

Day 107   Date: __ /__ /__   Hours: _____   Admin. Notes: _____

Reading/Literature: _____
Notes: _____
Writing/Language Arts: _____
Notes: _____
Mathematics: _____
Notes: _____
Science/Lab: _____
Notes: _____
US Hist./Govt./Civics: _____
Notes: _____
World History/Geography: _____
Notes: _____
Foreign Language: _____
Notes: _____
Sports/Fitness/Phys. Ed.: _____
Notes: _____
Music: _____
Notes: _____
Visual Arts: _____
Notes: _____
Performing Arts: _____
Notes: _____
Religious/Cultural Studies: _____
Notes: _____
Field Trips: _____
Notes: _____
Trade Skills/Shop: _____
Notes: _____
Health/Hygiene/Nutrition: _____
Notes: _____
Computers/Tech./Business Skills: _____
Notes: _____
Comm. Svc./Volunteerism/Career: _____
Notes: _____
Home Economics/Chores: _____
Notes: _____
Electives/Hobbies/Clubs: _____
Notes: _____
Miscellaneous: _____
_____

Day 108 Date: __ /__ /__ Hours: _____ Admin. Notes: _____

Reading/Literature: _____
Notes: _____
Writing/Language Arts: _____
Notes: _____
Mathematics: _____
Notes: _____
Science/Lab: _____
Notes: _____
US Hist./Govt./Civics: _____
Notes: _____
World History/Geography: _____
Notes: _____
Foreign Language: _____
Notes: _____
Sports/Fitness/Phys. Ed.: _____
Notes: _____
Music: _____
Notes: _____
Visual Arts: _____
Notes: _____
Performing Arts: _____
Notes: _____
Religious/Cultural Studies: _____
Notes: _____
Field Trips: _____
Notes: _____
Trade Skills/Shop: _____
Notes: _____
Health/Hygiene/Nutrition: _____
Notes: _____
Computers/Tech./Business Skills: _____
Notes: _____
Comm. Svc./Volunteerism/Career: _____
Notes: _____
Home Economics/Chores: _____
Notes: _____
Electives/Hobbies/Clubs: _____
Notes: _____
Miscellaneous: _____

Day 109 Date: __ /__ /__ Hours: _____ Admin. Notes:_____

Reading/Literature: _____
Notes: _____
Writing/Language Arts: _____
Notes: _____
Mathematics: _____
Notes: _____
Science/Lab: _____
Notes: _____
US Hist./Govt./Civics: _____
Notes: _____
World History/Geography: _____
Notes: _____
Foreign Language: _____
Notes: _____
Sports/Fitness/Phys. Ed.: _____
Notes: _____
Music: _____
Notes: _____
Visual Arts: _____
Notes: _____
Performing Arts: _____
Notes: _____
Religious/Cultural Studies: _____
Notes: _____
Field Trips: _____
Notes: _____
Trade Skills/Shop: _____
Notes: _____
Health/Hygiene/Nutrition: _____
Notes: _____
Computers/Tech./Business Skills: _____
Notes: _____
Comm. Svc./Volunteerism/Career: _____
Notes: _____
Home Economics/Chores: _____
Notes: _____
Electives/Hobbies/Clubs: _____
Notes: _____
Miscellaneous: _____

Day 110 Date: __ /__ /__ Hours: _____ Admin. Notes: _____

Reading/Literature: _____
  Notes: _____

Writing/Language Arts: _____
  Notes: _____

Mathematics: _____
  Notes: _____

Science/Lab: _____
  Notes: _____

US Hist./Govt./Civics: _____
  Notes: _____

World History/Geography: _____
  Notes: _____

Foreign Language: _____
  Notes: _____

Sports/Fitness/Phys. Ed.: _____
  Notes: _____

Music: _____
  Notes: _____

Visual Arts: _____
  Notes: _____

Performing Arts: _____
  Notes: _____

Religious/Cultural Studies: _____
  Notes: _____

Field Trips: _____
  Notes: _____

Trade Skills/Shop: _____
  Notes: _____

Health/Hygiene/Nutrition: _____
  Notes: _____

Computers/Tech./Business Skills: _____
  Notes: _____

Comm. Svc./Volunteerism/Career: _____
  Notes: _____

Home Economics/Chores: _____
  Notes: _____

Electives/Hobbies/Clubs: _____
  Notes: _____

Miscellaneous: _____
_____

Day 111   Date: __ /__ /__   Hours: _____   Admin. Notes: _____

Reading/Literature: _____
  Notes: _____
Writing/Language Arts: _____
  Notes: _____
Mathematics: _____
  Notes: _____
Science/Lab: _____
  Notes: _____
US Hist./Govt./Civics: _____
  Notes: _____
World History/Geography: _____
  Notes: _____
Foreign Language: _____
  Notes: _____
Sports/Fitness/Phys. Ed.: _____
  Notes: _____
Music: _____
  Notes: _____
Visual Arts: _____
  Notes: _____
Performing Arts: _____
  Notes: _____
Religious/Cultural Studies: _____
  Notes: _____
Field Trips: _____
  Notes: _____
Trade Skills/Shop: _____
  Notes: _____
Health/Hygiene/Nutrition: _____
  Notes: _____
Computers/Tech./Business Skills: _____
  Notes: _____
Comm. Svc./Volunteerism/Career: _____
  Notes: _____
Home Economics/Chores: _____
  Notes: _____
Electives/Hobbies/Clubs: _____
  Notes: _____
Miscellaneous: _____

Day 112   Date: __ /__ /__   Hours: _____   Admin. Notes: _____

Reading/Literature: _____
  Notes: _____
Writing/Language Arts: _____
  Notes: _____
Mathematics: _____
  Notes: _____
Science/Lab: _____
  Notes: _____
US Hist./Govt./Civics: _____
  Notes: _____
World History/Geography: _____
  Notes: _____
Foreign Language: _____
  Notes: _____
Sports/Fitness/Phys. Ed.: _____
  Notes: _____
Music: _____
  Notes: _____
Visual Arts: _____
  Notes: _____
Performing Arts: _____
  Notes: _____
Religious/Cultural Studies: _____
  Notes: _____
Field Trips: _____
  Notes: _____
Trade Skills/Shop: _____
  Notes: _____
Health/Hygiene/Nutrition: _____
  Notes: _____
Computers/Tech./Business Skills: _____
  Notes: _____
Comm. Svc./Volunteerism/Career: _____
  Notes: _____
Home Economics/Chores: _____
  Notes: _____
Electives/Hobbies/Clubs: _____
  Notes: _____
Miscellaneous: _____

Day 113 Date: __ /__ /__ Hours: _____ Admin. Notes:_____

Reading/Literature: _____
Notes: _____

Writing/Language Arts: _____
Notes: _____

Mathematics: _____
Notes: _____

Science/Lab: _____
Notes: _____

US Hist./Govt./Civics:_____
Notes: _____

World History/Geography: _____
Notes: _____

Foreign Language:_____
Notes: _____

Sports/Fitness/Phys. Ed.: _____
Notes: _____

Music: _____
Notes: _____

Visual Arts:_____
Notes: _____

Performing Arts: _____
Notes: _____

Religious/Cultural Studies: _____
Notes: _____

Field Trips: _____
Notes: _____

Trade Skills/Shop:_____
Notes: _____

Health/Hygiene/Nutrition: _____
Notes: _____

Computers/Tech./Business Skills: _____
Notes: _____

Comm. Svc./Volunteerism/Career:_____
Notes: _____

Home Economics/Chores: _____
Notes: _____

Electives/Hobbies/Clubs:_____
Notes: _____

Miscellaneous: _____

Day 114   Date: __ / __ / __   Hours: _____   Admin. Notes: _____

Reading/Literature: _____
   Notes: _____

Writing/Language Arts: _____
   Notes: _____

Mathematics: _____
   Notes: _____

Science/Lab: _____
   Notes: _____

US Hist./Govt./Civics: _____
   Notes: _____

World History/Geography: _____
   Notes: _____

Foreign Language: _____
   Notes: _____

Sports/Fitness/Phys. Ed.: _____
   Notes: _____

Music: _____
   Notes: _____

Visual Arts: _____
   Notes: _____

Performing Arts: _____
   Notes: _____

Religious/Cultural Studies: _____
   Notes: _____

Field Trips: _____
   Notes: _____

Trade Skills/Shop: _____
   Notes: _____

Health/Hygiene/Nutrition: _____
   Notes: _____

Computers/Tech./Business Skills: _____
   Notes: _____

Comm. Svc./Volunteerism/Career: _____
   Notes: _____

Home Economics/Chores: _____
   Notes: _____

Electives/Hobbies/Clubs: _____
   Notes: _____

Miscellaneous: _____
_____

Day 115   Date: __ /__ /__   Hours: _____   Admin. Notes:_____

Reading/Literature: _____
Notes: _____

Writing/Language Arts: _____
Notes: _____

Mathematics: _____
Notes: _____

Science/Lab: _____
Notes: _____

US Hist./Govt./Civics:_____
Notes: _____

World History/Geography: _____
Notes: _____

Foreign Language: _____
Notes: _____

Sports/Fitness/Phys. Ed.: _____
Notes: _____

Music: _____
Notes: _____

Visual Arts:_____
Notes: _____

Performing Arts: _____
Notes: _____

Religious/Cultural Studies: _____
Notes: _____

Field Trips: _____
Notes: _____

Trade Skills/Shop:_____
Notes: _____

Health/Hygiene/Nutrition: _____
Notes: _____

Computers/Tech./Business Skills: _____
Notes: _____

Comm. Svc./Volunteerism/Career:_____
Notes: _____

Home Economics/Chores: _____
Notes: _____

Electives/Hobbies/Clubs:_____
Notes: _____

Miscellaneous: _____

Day 116   Date: __ /__ /__   Hours: _____   Admin. Notes: _____

Reading/Literature: _____
Notes: _____
Writing/Language Arts: _____
Notes: _____
Mathematics: _____
Notes: _____
Science/Lab: _____
Notes: _____
US Hist./Govt./Civics: _____
Notes: _____
World History/Geography: _____
Notes: _____
Foreign Language: _____
Notes: _____
Sports/Fitness/Phys. Ed.: _____
Notes: _____
Music: _____
Notes: _____
Visual Arts: _____
Notes: _____
Performing Arts: _____
Notes: _____
Religious/Cultural Studies: _____
Notes: _____
Field Trips: _____
Notes: _____
Trade Skills/Shop: _____
Notes: _____
Health/Hygiene/Nutrition: _____
Notes: _____
Computers/Tech./Business Skills: _____
Notes: _____
Comm. Svc./Volunteerism/Career: _____
Notes: _____
Home Economics/Chores: _____
Notes: _____
Electives/Hobbies/Clubs: _____
Notes: _____
Miscellaneous: _____
_____

Day 117 Date: __ / __ / __ Hours: _____ Admin. Notes: _____

Reading/Literature: _____
   Notes: _____

Writing/Language Arts: _____
   Notes: _____

Mathematics: _____
   Notes: _____

Science/Lab: _____
   Notes: _____

US Hist./Govt./Civics: _____
   Notes: _____

World History/Geography: _____
   Notes: _____

Foreign Language: _____
   Notes: _____

Sports/Fitness/Phys. Ed.: _____
   Notes: _____

Music: _____
   Notes: _____

Visual Arts: _____
   Notes: _____

Performing Arts: _____
   Notes: _____

Religious/Cultural Studies: _____
   Notes: _____

Field Trips: _____
   Notes: _____

Trade Skills/Shop: _____
   Notes: _____

Health/Hygiene/Nutrition: _____
   Notes: _____

Computers/Tech./Business Skills: _____
   Notes: _____

Comm. Svc./Volunteerism/Career: _____
   Notes: _____

Home Economics/Chores: _____
   Notes: _____

Electives/Hobbies/Clubs: _____
   Notes: _____

Miscellaneous: _____
_____

Day 118   Date: __ /__ /__   Hours: _____   Admin. Notes: _____

Reading/Literature: _____
   Notes: _____

Writing/Language Arts: _____
   Notes: _____

Mathematics: _____
   Notes: _____

Science/Lab: _____
   Notes: _____

US Hist./Govt./Civics: _____
   Notes: _____

World History/Geography: _____
   Notes: _____

Foreign Language: _____
   Notes: _____

Sports/Fitness/Phys. Ed.: _____
   Notes: _____

Music: _____
   Notes: _____

Visual Arts: _____
   Notes: _____

Performing Arts: _____
   Notes: _____

Religious/Cultural Studies: _____
   Notes: _____

Field Trips: _____
   Notes: _____

Trade Skills/Shop: _____
   Notes: _____

Health/Hygiene/Nutrition: _____
   Notes: _____

Computers/Tech./Business Skills: _____
   Notes: _____

Comm. Svc./Volunteerism/Career: _____
   Notes: _____

Home Economics/Chores: _____
   Notes: _____

Electives/Hobbies/Clubs: _____
   Notes: _____

Miscellaneous: _____
_____

Day 119   Date: __ /__ /__   Hours: _____   Admin. Notes: _____

Reading/Literature: _____
Notes: _____
Writing/Language Arts: _____
Notes: _____
Mathematics: _____
Notes: _____
Science/Lab: _____
Notes: _____
US Hist./Govt./Civics: _____
Notes: _____
World History/Geography: _____
Notes: _____
Foreign Language: _____
Notes: _____
Sports/Fitness/Phys. Ed.: _____
Notes: _____
Music: _____
Notes: _____
Visual Arts: _____
Notes: _____
Performing Arts: _____
Notes: _____
Religious/Cultural Studies: _____
Notes: _____
Field Trips: _____
Notes: _____
Trade Skills/Shop: _____
Notes: _____
Health/Hygiene/Nutrition: _____
Notes: _____
Computers/Tech./Business Skills: _____
Notes: _____
Comm. Svc./Volunteerism/Career: _____
Notes: _____
Home Economics/Chores: _____
Notes: _____
Electives/Hobbies/Clubs: _____
Notes: _____
Miscellaneous: _____

Day 120   Date: __ /__ /__   Hours: _____   Admin. Notes: _____

Reading/Literature: _____
  Notes: _____

Writing/Language Arts: _____
  Notes: _____

Mathematics: _____
  Notes: _____

Science/Lab: _____
  Notes: _____

US Hist./Govt./Civics: _____
  Notes: _____

World History/Geography: _____
  Notes: _____

Foreign Language: _____
  Notes: _____

Sports/Fitness/Phys. Ed.: _____
  Notes: _____

Music: _____
  Notes: _____

Visual Arts: _____
  Notes: _____

Performing Arts: _____
  Notes: _____

Religious/Cultural Studies: _____
  Notes: _____

Field Trips: _____
  Notes: _____

Trade Skills/Shop: _____
  Notes: _____

Health/Hygiene/Nutrition: _____
  Notes: _____

Computers/Tech./Business Skills: _____
  Notes: _____

Comm. Svc./Volunteerism/Career: _____
  Notes: _____

Home Economics/Chores: _____
  Notes: _____

Electives/Hobbies/Clubs: _____
  Notes: _____

Miscellaneous: _____

Day 121 Date: __ /__ /__ Hours: _____ Admin. Notes:_____

Reading/Literature: _____
  Notes: _____
Writing/Language Arts: _____
  Notes: _____
Mathematics: _____
  Notes: _____
Science/Lab: _____
  Notes: _____
US Hist./Govt./Civics: _____
  Notes: _____
World History/Geography: _____
  Notes: _____
Foreign Language: _____
  Notes: _____
Sports/Fitness/Phys. Ed.: _____
  Notes: _____
Music: _____
  Notes: _____
Visual Arts: _____
  Notes: _____
Performing Arts: _____
  Notes: _____
Religious/Cultural Studies: _____
  Notes: _____
Field Trips: _____
  Notes: _____
Trade Skills/Shop: _____
  Notes: _____
Health/Hygiene/Nutrition: _____
  Notes: _____
Computers/Tech./Business Skills: _____
  Notes: _____
Comm. Svc./Volunteerism/Career: _____
  Notes: _____
Home Economics/Chores: _____
  Notes: _____
Electives/Hobbies/Clubs: _____
  Notes: _____
Miscellaneous: _____
_____

Day 122 Date: __ /__ /__ Hours: _____ Admin. Notes: _____

Reading/Literature: _____
Notes: _____
Writing/Language Arts: _____
Notes: _____
Mathematics: _____
Notes: _____
Science/Lab: _____
Notes: _____
US Hist./Govt./Civics: _____
Notes: _____
World History/Geography: _____
Notes: _____
Foreign Language: _____
Notes: _____
Sports/Fitness/Phys. Ed.: _____
Notes: _____
Music: _____
Notes: _____
Visual Arts: _____
Notes: _____
Performing Arts: _____
Notes: _____
Religious/Cultural Studies: _____
Notes: _____
Field Trips: _____
Notes: _____
Trade Skills/Shop: _____
Notes: _____
Health/Hygiene/Nutrition: _____
Notes: _____
Computers/Tech./Business Skills: _____
Notes: _____
Comm. Svc./Volunteerism/Career: _____
Notes: _____
Home Economics/Chores: _____
Notes: _____
Electives/Hobbies/Clubs: _____
Notes: _____
Miscellaneous: _____

Day 123   Date: __ /__ /__   Hours: _____   Admin. Notes: _____

Reading/Literature: _____
  Notes: _____
Writing/Language Arts: _____
  Notes: _____
Mathematics: _____
  Notes: _____
Science/Lab: _____
  Notes: _____
US Hist./Govt./Civics: _____
  Notes: _____
World History/Geography: _____
  Notes: _____
Foreign Language: _____
  Notes: _____
Sports/Fitness/Phys. Ed.: _____
  Notes: _____
Music: _____
  Notes: _____
Visual Arts: _____
  Notes: _____
Performing Arts: _____
  Notes: _____
Religious/Cultural Studies: _____
  Notes: _____
Field Trips: _____
  Notes: _____
Trade Skills/Shop: _____
  Notes: _____
Health/Hygiene/Nutrition: _____
  Notes: _____
Computers/Tech./Business Skills: _____
  Notes: _____
Comm. Svc./Volunteerism/Career: _____
  Notes: _____
Home Economics/Chores: _____
  Notes: _____
Electives/Hobbies/Clubs: _____
  Notes: _____
Miscellaneous: _____

Day 124 Date: __ /__ /__ Hours: _____ Admin. Notes: _____

Reading/Literature: _____
   Notes: _____

Writing/Language Arts: _____
   Notes: _____

Mathematics: _____
   Notes: _____

Science/Lab: _____
   Notes: _____

US Hist./Govt./Civics: _____
   Notes: _____

World History/Geography: _____
   Notes: _____

Foreign Language: _____
   Notes: _____

Sports/Fitness/Phys. Ed.: _____
   Notes: _____

Music: _____
   Notes: _____

Visual Arts: _____
   Notes: _____

Performing Arts: _____
   Notes: _____

Religious/Cultural Studies: _____
   Notes: _____

Field Trips: _____
   Notes: _____

Trade Skills/Shop: _____
   Notes: _____

Health/Hygiene/Nutrition: _____
   Notes: _____

Computers/Tech./Business Skills: _____
   Notes: _____

Comm. Svc./Volunteerism/Career: _____
   Notes: _____

Home Economics/Chores: _____
   Notes: _____

Electives/Hobbies/Clubs: _____
   Notes: _____

Miscellaneous: _____
_____

Day 125 Date: __ /__ /__ Hours: _____ Admin. Notes:_____

Reading/Literature: _____
Notes: _____

Writing/Language Arts: _____
Notes: _____

Mathematics: _____
Notes: _____

Science/Lab: _____
Notes: _____

US Hist./Govt./Civics: _____
Notes: _____

World History/Geography: _____
Notes: _____

Foreign Language: _____
Notes: _____

Sports/Fitness/Phys. Ed.: _____
Notes: _____

Music: _____
Notes: _____

Visual Arts: _____
Notes: _____

Performing Arts: _____
Notes: _____

Religious/Cultural Studies: _____
Notes: _____

Field Trips: _____
Notes: _____

Trade Skills/Shop: _____
Notes: _____

Health/Hygiene/Nutrition: _____
Notes: _____

Computers/Tech./Business Skills: _____
Notes: _____

Comm. Svc./Volunteerism/Career: _____
Notes: _____

Home Economics/Chores: _____
Notes: _____

Electives/Hobbies/Clubs: _____
Notes: _____

Miscellaneous: _____
_____

Day 126 Date: __ /__ /__ Hours: _____ Admin. Notes: _____

Reading/Literature: _____
  Notes: _____
Writing/Language Arts: _____
  Notes: _____
Mathematics: _____
  Notes: _____
Science/Lab: _____
  Notes: _____
US Hist./Govt./Civics: _____
  Notes: _____
World History/Geography: _____
  Notes: _____
Foreign Language: _____
  Notes: _____
Sports/Fitness/Phys. Ed.: _____
  Notes: _____
Music: _____
  Notes: _____
Visual Arts: _____
  Notes: _____
Performing Arts: _____
  Notes: _____
Religious/Cultural Studies: _____
  Notes: _____
Field Trips: _____
  Notes: _____
Trade Skills/Shop: _____
  Notes: _____
Health/Hygiene/Nutrition: _____
  Notes: _____
Computers/Tech./Business Skills: _____
  Notes: _____
Comm. Svc./Volunteerism/Career: _____
  Notes: _____
Home Economics/Chores: _____
  Notes: _____
Electives/Hobbies/Clubs: _____
  Notes: _____
Miscellaneous: _____

Day 127   Date: __ /__ /__   Hours: _____   Admin. Notes: _____

Reading/Literature: _____
Notes: _____

Writing/Language Arts: _____
Notes: _____

Mathematics: _____
Notes: _____

Science/Lab: _____
Notes: _____

US Hist./Govt./Civics: _____
Notes: _____

World History/Geography: _____
Notes: _____

Foreign Language: _____
Notes: _____

Sports/Fitness/Phys. Ed.: _____
Notes: _____

Music: _____
Notes: _____

Visual Arts: _____
Notes: _____

Performing Arts: _____
Notes: _____

Religious/Cultural Studies: _____
Notes: _____

Field Trips: _____
Notes: _____

Trade Skills/Shop: _____
Notes: _____

Health/Hygiene/Nutrition: _____
Notes: _____

Computers/Tech./Business Skills: _____
Notes: _____

Comm. Svc./Volunteerism/Career: _____
Notes: _____

Home Economics/Chores: _____
Notes: _____

Electives/Hobbies/Clubs: _____
Notes: _____

Miscellaneous: _____
_____

Day 128   Date: __ / __ / __   Hours: _____   Admin. Notes: _____

Reading/Literature: _____
   Notes: _____

Writing/Language Arts: _____
   Notes: _____

Mathematics: _____
   Notes: _____

Science/Lab: _____
   Notes: _____

US Hist./Govt./Civics: _____
   Notes: _____

World History/Geography: _____
   Notes: _____

Foreign Language: _____
   Notes: _____

Sports/Fitness/Phys. Ed.: _____
   Notes: _____

Music: _____
   Notes: _____

Visual Arts: _____
   Notes: _____

Performing Arts: _____
   Notes: _____

Religious/Cultural Studies: _____
   Notes: _____

Field Trips: _____
   Notes: _____

Trade Skills/Shop: _____
   Notes: _____

Health/Hygiene/Nutrition: _____
   Notes: _____

Computers/Tech./Business Skills: _____
   Notes: _____

Comm. Svc./Volunteerism/Career: _____
   Notes: _____

Home Economics/Chores: _____
   Notes: _____

Electives/Hobbies/Clubs: _____
   Notes: _____

Miscellaneous: _____

Day 129 Date: __ /__ /__ Hours: _____ Admin. Notes:_____

Reading/Literature: _____
Notes: _____
Writing/Language Arts: _____
Notes: _____
Mathematics: _____
Notes: _____
Science/Lab: _____
Notes: _____
US Hist./Govt./Civics: _____
Notes: _____
World History/Geography: _____
Notes: _____
Foreign Language: _____
Notes: _____
Sports/Fitness/Phys. Ed.: _____
Notes: _____
Music: _____
Notes: _____
Visual Arts: _____
Notes: _____
Performing Arts: _____
Notes: _____
Religious/Cultural Studies: _____
Notes: _____
Field Trips: _____
Notes: _____
Trade Skills/Shop: _____
Notes: _____
Health/Hygiene/Nutrition: _____
Notes: _____
Computers/Tech./Business Skills: _____
Notes: _____
Comm. Svc./Volunteerism/Career: _____
Notes: _____
Home Economics/Chores: _____
Notes: _____
Electives/Hobbies/Clubs: _____
Notes: _____
Miscellaneous: _____
_____

Day 130 Date: __ / __ / __ Hours: _____ Admin. Notes: _____

Reading/Literature: _____
  Notes: _____

Writing/Language Arts: _____
  Notes: _____

Mathematics: _____
  Notes: _____

Science/Lab: _____
  Notes: _____

US Hist./Govt./Civics: _____
  Notes: _____

World History/Geography: _____
  Notes: _____

Foreign Language: _____
  Notes: _____

Sports/Fitness/Phys. Ed.: _____
  Notes: _____

Music: _____
  Notes: _____

Visual Arts: _____
  Notes: _____

Performing Arts: _____
  Notes: _____

Religious/Cultural Studies: _____
  Notes: _____

Field Trips: _____
  Notes: _____

Trade Skills/Shop: _____
  Notes: _____

Health/Hygiene/Nutrition: _____
  Notes: _____

Computers/Tech./Business Skills: _____
  Notes: _____

Comm. Svc./Volunteerism/Career: _____
  Notes: _____

Home Economics/Chores: _____
  Notes: _____

Electives/Hobbies/Clubs: _____
  Notes: _____

Miscellaneous: _____

Day 131 Date: __ /__ /__ Hours: _____ Admin. Notes: _____

Reading/Literature: _____
 Notes: _____
Writing/Language Arts: _____
 Notes: _____
Mathematics: _____
 Notes: _____
Science/Lab: _____
 Notes: _____
US Hist./Govt./Civics: _____
 Notes: _____
World History/Geography: _____
 Notes: _____
Foreign Language: _____
 Notes: _____
Sports/Fitness/Phys. Ed.: _____
 Notes: _____
Music: _____
 Notes: _____
Visual Arts: _____
 Notes: _____
Performing Arts: _____
 Notes: _____
Religious/Cultural Studies: _____
 Notes: _____
Field Trips: _____
 Notes: _____
Trade Skills/Shop: _____
 Notes: _____
Health/Hygiene/Nutrition: _____
 Notes: _____
Computers/Tech./Business Skills: _____
 Notes: _____
Comm. Svc./Volunteerism/Career: _____
 Notes: _____
Home Economics/Chores: _____
 Notes: _____
Electives/Hobbies/Clubs: _____
 Notes: _____
Miscellaneous: _____

Day 132   Date: __ /__ /__   Hours: _____   Admin. Notes: _____

Reading/Literature: _____
   Notes: _____
Writing/Language Arts: _____
   Notes: _____
Mathematics: _____
   Notes: _____
Science/Lab: _____
   Notes: _____
US Hist./Govt./Civics: _____
   Notes: _____
World History/Geography: _____
   Notes: _____
Foreign Language: _____
   Notes: _____
Sports/Fitness/Phys. Ed.: _____
   Notes: _____
Music: _____
   Notes: _____
Visual Arts: _____
   Notes: _____
Performing Arts: _____
   Notes: _____
Religious/Cultural Studies: _____
   Notes: _____
Field Trips: _____
   Notes: _____
Trade Skills/Shop: _____
   Notes: _____
Health/Hygiene/Nutrition: _____
   Notes: _____
Computers/Tech./Business Skills: _____
   Notes: _____
Comm. Svc./Volunteerism/Career: _____
   Notes: _____
Home Economics/Chores: _____
   Notes: _____
Electives/Hobbies/Clubs: _____
   Notes: _____
Miscellaneous: _____

Day 133 Date: __ /__ /__ Hours: _____ Admin. Notes: _____

Reading/Literature: _____
Notes: _____

Writing/Language Arts: _____
Notes: _____

Mathematics: _____
Notes: _____

Science/Lab: _____
Notes: _____

US Hist./Govt./Civics: _____
Notes: _____

World History/Geography: _____
Notes: _____

Foreign Language: _____
Notes: _____

Sports/Fitness/Phys. Ed.: _____
Notes: _____

Music: _____
Notes: _____

Visual Arts: _____
Notes: _____

Performing Arts: _____
Notes: _____

Religious/Cultural Studies: _____
Notes: _____

Field Trips: _____
Notes: _____

Trade Skills/Shop: _____
Notes: _____

Health/Hygiene/Nutrition: _____
Notes: _____

Computers/Tech./Business Skills: _____
Notes: _____

Comm. Svc./Volunteerism/Career: _____
Notes: _____

Home Economics/Chores: _____
Notes: _____

Electives/Hobbies/Clubs: _____
Notes: _____

Miscellaneous: _____
_____

Day 134   Date: __ /__ /__   Hours: _____   Admin. Notes: _____

Reading/Literature: _____
  Notes: _____
Writing/Language Arts: _____
  Notes: _____
Mathematics: _____
  Notes: _____
Science/Lab: _____
  Notes: _____
US Hist./Govt./Civics: _____
  Notes: _____
World History/Geography: _____
  Notes: _____
Foreign Language: _____
  Notes: _____
Sports/Fitness/Phys. Ed.: _____
  Notes: _____
Music: _____
  Notes: _____
Visual Arts: _____
  Notes: _____
Performing Arts: _____
  Notes: _____
Religious/Cultural Studies: _____
  Notes: _____
Field Trips: _____
  Notes: _____
Trade Skills/Shop: _____
  Notes: _____
Health/Hygiene/Nutrition: _____
  Notes: _____
Computers/Tech./Business Skills: _____
  Notes: _____
Comm. Svc./Volunteerism/Career: _____
  Notes: _____
Home Economics/Chores: _____
  Notes: _____
Electives/Hobbies/Clubs: _____
  Notes: _____
Miscellaneous: _____
_____

Day 135 Date: __ /__ /__ Hours: _____ Admin. Notes:_____

Reading/Literature: _____
  Notes: _____
Writing/Language Arts: _____
  Notes: _____
Mathematics: _____
  Notes: _____
Science/Lab: _____
  Notes: _____
US Hist./Govt./Civics: _____
  Notes: _____
World History/Geography: _____
  Notes: _____
Foreign Language: _____
  Notes: _____
Sports/Fitness/Phys. Ed.: _____
  Notes: _____
Music: _____
  Notes: _____
Visual Arts: _____
  Notes: _____
Performing Arts: _____
  Notes: _____
Religious/Cultural Studies: _____
  Notes: _____
Field Trips: _____
  Notes: _____
Trade Skills/Shop: _____
  Notes: _____
Health/Hygiene/Nutrition: _____
  Notes: _____
Computers/Tech./Business Skills: _____
  Notes: _____
Comm. Svc./Volunteerism/Career: _____
  Notes: _____
Home Economics/Chores: _____
  Notes: _____
Electives/Hobbies/Clubs: _____
  Notes: _____
Miscellaneous: _____

Day 136 Date: __ /__ /__ Hours: _____ Admin. Notes: _____

Reading/Literature: _____
Notes: _____
Writing/Language Arts: _____
Notes: _____
Mathematics: _____
Notes: _____
Science/Lab: _____
Notes: _____
US Hist./Govt./Civics: _____
Notes: _____
World History/Geography: _____
Notes: _____
Foreign Language: _____
Notes: _____
Sports/Fitness/Phys. Ed.: _____
Notes: _____
Music: _____
Notes: _____
Visual Arts: _____
Notes: _____
Performing Arts: _____
Notes: _____
Religious/Cultural Studies: _____
Notes: _____
Field Trips: _____
Notes: _____
Trade Skills/Shop: _____
Notes: _____
Health/Hygiene/Nutrition: _____
Notes: _____
Computers/Tech./Business Skills: _____
Notes: _____
Comm. Svc./Volunteerism/Career: _____
Notes: _____
Home Economics/Chores: _____
Notes: _____
Electives/Hobbies/Clubs: _____
Notes: _____
Miscellaneous: _____

Day 137 Date: __ /__ /__ Hours: _____ Admin. Notes: _____

Reading/Literature: _____
Notes: _____

Writing/Language Arts: _____
Notes: _____

Mathematics: _____
Notes: _____

Science/Lab: _____
Notes: _____

US Hist./Govt./Civics: _____
Notes: _____

World History/Geography: _____
Notes: _____

Foreign Language: _____
Notes: _____

Sports/Fitness/Phys. Ed.: _____
Notes: _____

Music: _____
Notes: _____

Visual Arts: _____
Notes: _____

Performing Arts: _____
Notes: _____

Religious/Cultural Studies: _____
Notes: _____

Field Trips: _____
Notes: _____

Trade Skills/Shop: _____
Notes: _____

Health/Hygiene/Nutrition: _____
Notes: _____

Computers/Tech./Business Skills: _____
Notes: _____

Comm. Svc./Volunteerism/Career: _____
Notes: _____

Home Economics/Chores: _____
Notes: _____

Electives/Hobbies/Clubs: _____
Notes: _____

Miscellaneous: _____

Day 138   Date: __ /__ /__   Hours: _____   Admin. Notes: _____

Reading/Literature: _____
  Notes: _____
Writing/Language Arts: _____
  Notes: _____
Mathematics: _____
  Notes: _____
Science/Lab: _____
  Notes: _____
US Hist./Govt./Civics: _____
  Notes: _____
World History/Geography: _____
  Notes: _____
Foreign Language: _____
  Notes: _____
Sports/Fitness/Phys. Ed.: _____
  Notes: _____
Music: _____
  Notes: _____
Visual Arts: _____
  Notes: _____
Performing Arts: _____
  Notes: _____
Religious/Cultural Studies: _____
  Notes: _____
Field Trips: _____
  Notes: _____
Trade Skills/Shop: _____
  Notes: _____
Health/Hygiene/Nutrition: _____
  Notes: _____
Computers/Tech./Business Skills: _____
  Notes: _____
Comm. Svc./Volunteerism/Career: _____
  Notes: _____
Home Economics/Chores: _____
  Notes: _____
Electives/Hobbies/Clubs: _____
  Notes: _____
Miscellaneous: _____
_____

Day 139 Date: __ /__ /__ Hours: _____ Admin. Notes: _____

Reading/Literature: _____
  Notes: _____
Writing/Language Arts: _____
  Notes: _____
Mathematics: _____
  Notes: _____
Science/Lab: _____
  Notes: _____
US Hist./Govt./Civics: _____
  Notes: _____
World History/Geography: _____
  Notes: _____
Foreign Language: _____
  Notes: _____
Sports/Fitness/Phys. Ed.: _____
  Notes: _____
Music: _____
  Notes: _____
Visual Arts: _____
  Notes: _____
Performing Arts: _____
  Notes: _____
Religious/Cultural Studies: _____
  Notes: _____
Field Trips: _____
  Notes: _____
Trade Skills/Shop: _____
  Notes: _____
Health/Hygiene/Nutrition: _____
  Notes: _____
Computers/Tech./Business Skills: _____
  Notes: _____
Comm. Svc./Volunteerism/Career: _____
  Notes: _____
Home Economics/Chores: _____
  Notes: _____
Electives/Hobbies/Clubs: _____
  Notes: _____
Miscellaneous: _____

Day 140 Date: __ /__ /__ Hours: _____ Admin. Notes: _____

Reading/Literature: _____
   Notes: _____
Writing/Language Arts: _____
   Notes: _____
Mathematics: _____
   Notes: _____
Science/Lab: _____
   Notes: _____
US Hist./Govt./Civics: _____
   Notes: _____
World History/Geography: _____
   Notes: _____
Foreign Language: _____
   Notes: _____
Sports/Fitness/Phys. Ed.: _____
   Notes: _____
Music: _____
   Notes: _____
Visual Arts: _____
   Notes: _____
Performing Arts: _____
   Notes: _____
Religious/Cultural Studies: _____
   Notes: _____
Field Trips: _____
   Notes: _____
Trade Skills/Shop: _____
   Notes: _____
Health/Hygiene/Nutrition: _____
   Notes: _____
Computers/Tech./Business Skills: _____
   Notes: _____
Comm. Svc./Volunteerism/Career: _____
   Notes: _____
Home Economics/Chores: _____
   Notes: _____
Electives/Hobbies/Clubs: _____
   Notes: _____
Miscellaneous: _____

Day 141 Date: __ /__ /__ Hours: _____ Admin. Notes:_____

Reading/Literature: _____
Notes: _____
Writing/Language Arts: _____
Notes: _____
Mathematics: _____
Notes: _____
Science/Lab: _____
Notes: _____
US Hist./Govt./Civics:_____
Notes: _____
World History/Geography: _____
Notes: _____
Foreign Language:_____
Notes: _____
Sports/Fitness/Phys. Ed.: _____
Notes: _____
Music: _____
Notes: _____
Visual Arts:_____
Notes: _____
Performing Arts: _____
Notes: _____
Religious/Cultural Studies:_____
Notes: _____
Field Trips: _____
Notes: _____
Trade Skills/Shop:_____
Notes: _____
Health/Hygiene/Nutrition: _____
Notes: _____
Computers/Tech./Business Skills: _____
Notes: _____
Comm. Svc./Volunteerism/Career:_____
Notes: _____
Home Economics/Chores: _____
Notes: _____
Electives/Hobbies/Clubs:_____
Notes: _____
Miscellaneous: _____

Day 142 Date: __ /__ /__ Hours: _____ Admin. Notes: _____

Reading/Literature: _____
Notes: _____
Writing/Language Arts: _____
Notes: _____
Mathematics: _____
Notes: _____
Science/Lab: _____
Notes: _____
US Hist./Govt./Civics: _____
Notes: _____
World History/Geography: _____
Notes: _____
Foreign Language: _____
Notes: _____
Sports/Fitness/Phys. Ed.: _____
Notes: _____
Music: _____
Notes: _____
Visual Arts: _____
Notes: _____
Performing Arts: _____
Notes: _____
Religious/Cultural Studies: _____
Notes: _____
Field Trips: _____
Notes: _____
Trade Skills/Shop: _____
Notes: _____
Health/Hygiene/Nutrition: _____
Notes: _____
Computers/Tech./Business Skills: _____
Notes: _____
Comm. Svc./Volunteerism/Career: _____
Notes: _____
Home Economics/Chores: _____
Notes: _____
Electives/Hobbies/Clubs: _____
Notes: _____
Miscellaneous: _____
_____

Day 143   Date: __ /__ /__   Hours: _____   Admin. Notes:_____

Reading/Literature: _____
  Notes: _____

Writing/Language Arts: _____
  Notes: _____

Mathematics: _____
  Notes: _____

Science/Lab: _____
  Notes: _____

US Hist./Govt./Civics:_____
  Notes: _____

World History/Geography: _____
  Notes: _____

Foreign Language: _____
  Notes: _____

Sports/Fitness/Phys. Ed.: _____
  Notes: _____

Music: _____
  Notes: _____

Visual Arts:_____
  Notes: _____

Performing Arts: _____
  Notes: _____

Religious/Cultural Studies: _____
  Notes: _____

Field Trips: _____
  Notes: _____

Trade Skills/Shop:_____
  Notes: _____

Health/Hygiene/Nutrition: _____
  Notes: _____

Computers/Tech./Business Skills: _____
  Notes: _____

Comm. Svc./Volunteerism/Career:_____
  Notes: _____

Home Economics/Chores: _____
  Notes: _____

Electives/Hobbies/Clubs:_____
  Notes: _____

Miscellaneous: _____

Day 144 Date: __ /__ /__ Hours: _____ Admin. Notes: _____

Reading/Literature: _____
 Notes: _____
Writing/Language Arts: _____
 Notes: _____
Mathematics: _____
 Notes: _____
Science/Lab: _____
 Notes: _____
US Hist./Govt./Civics: _____
 Notes: _____
World History/Geography: _____
 Notes: _____
Foreign Language: _____
 Notes: _____
Sports/Fitness/Phys. Ed.: _____
 Notes: _____
Music: _____
 Notes: _____
Visual Arts: _____
 Notes: _____
Performing Arts: _____
 Notes: _____
Religious/Cultural Studies: _____
 Notes: _____
Field Trips: _____
 Notes: _____
Trade Skills/Shop: _____
 Notes: _____
Health/Hygiene/Nutrition: _____
 Notes: _____
Computers/Tech./Business Skills: _____
 Notes: _____
Comm. Svc./Volunteerism/Career: _____
 Notes: _____
Home Economics/Chores: _____
 Notes: _____
Electives/Hobbies/Clubs: _____
 Notes: _____
Miscellaneous: _____
_____

Day 145   Date: __ /__ /__   Hours: _____   Admin. Notes:_____

Reading/Literature: _____
   Notes: _____
Writing/Language Arts: _____
   Notes: _____
Mathematics: _____
   Notes: _____
Science/Lab: _____
   Notes: _____
US Hist./Govt./Civics: _____
   Notes: _____
World History/Geography: _____
   Notes: _____
Foreign Language: _____
   Notes: _____
Sports/Fitness/Phys. Ed.: _____
   Notes: _____
Music: _____
   Notes: _____
Visual Arts: _____
   Notes: _____
Performing Arts: _____
   Notes: _____
Religious/Cultural Studies: _____
   Notes: _____
Field Trips: _____
   Notes: _____
Trade Skills/Shop: _____
   Notes: _____
Health/Hygiene/Nutrition: _____
   Notes: _____
Computers/Tech./Business Skills: _____
   Notes: _____
Comm. Svc./Volunteerism/Career: _____
   Notes: _____
Home Economics/Chores: _____
   Notes: _____
Electives/Hobbies/Clubs: _____
   Notes: _____
Miscellaneous: _____
   _____

Day 146 Date: __ /__ /__ Hours: _____ Admin. Notes: _____

Reading/Literature: _____
Notes: _____

Writing/Language Arts: _____
Notes: _____

Mathematics: _____
Notes: _____

Science/Lab: _____
Notes: _____

US Hist./Govt./Civics: _____
Notes: _____

World History/Geography: _____
Notes: _____

Foreign Language: _____
Notes: _____

Sports/Fitness/Phys. Ed.: _____
Notes: _____

Music: _____
Notes: _____

Visual Arts: _____
Notes: _____

Performing Arts: _____
Notes: _____

Religious/Cultural Studies: _____
Notes: _____

Field Trips: _____
Notes: _____

Trade Skills/Shop: _____
Notes: _____

Health/Hygiene/Nutrition: _____
Notes: _____

Computers/Tech./Business Skills: _____
Notes: _____

Comm. Svc./Volunteerism/Career: _____
Notes: _____

Home Economics/Chores: _____
Notes: _____

Electives/Hobbies/Clubs: _____
Notes: _____

Miscellaneous: _____

Day 147   Date: __ /__ /__   Hours: _____   Admin. Notes: _____

Reading/Literature: _____
   Notes: _____
Writing/Language Arts: _____
   Notes: _____
Mathematics: _____
   Notes: _____
Science/Lab: _____
   Notes: _____
US Hist./Govt./Civics: _____
   Notes: _____
World History/Geography: _____
   Notes: _____
Foreign Language: _____
   Notes: _____
Sports/Fitness/Phys. Ed.: _____
   Notes: _____
Music: _____
   Notes: _____
Visual Arts: _____
   Notes: _____
Performing Arts: _____
   Notes: _____
Religious/Cultural Studies: _____
   Notes: _____
Field Trips: _____
   Notes: _____
Trade Skills/Shop: _____
   Notes: _____
Health/Hygiene/Nutrition: _____
   Notes: _____
Computers/Tech./Business Skills: _____
   Notes: _____
Comm. Svc./Volunteerism/Career: _____
   Notes: _____
Home Economics/Chores: _____
   Notes: _____
Electives/Hobbies/Clubs: _____
   Notes: _____
Miscellaneous: _____

Day 148 Date: __ / __ / __ Hours: _____ Admin. Notes: _____

Reading/Literature: _____
Notes: _____

Writing/Language Arts: _____
Notes: _____

Mathematics: _____
Notes: _____

Science/Lab: _____
Notes: _____

US Hist./Govt./Civics: _____
Notes: _____

World History/Geography: _____
Notes: _____

Foreign Language: _____
Notes: _____

Sports/Fitness/Phys. Ed.: _____
Notes: _____

Music: _____
Notes: _____

Visual Arts: _____
Notes: _____

Performing Arts: _____
Notes: _____

Religious/Cultural Studies: _____
Notes: _____

Field Trips: _____
Notes: _____

Trade Skills/Shop: _____
Notes: _____

Health/Hygiene/Nutrition: _____
Notes: _____

Computers/Tech./Business Skills: _____
Notes: _____

Comm. Svc./Volunteerism/Career: _____
Notes: _____

Home Economics/Chores: _____
Notes: _____

Electives/Hobbies/Clubs: _____
Notes: _____

Miscellaneous: _____

Day 149 Date: __ /__ /__ Hours: _____ Admin. Notes: _____

Reading/Literature: _____
   Notes: _____
Writing/Language Arts: _____
   Notes: _____
Mathematics: _____
   Notes: _____
Science/Lab: _____
   Notes: _____
US Hist./Govt./Civics: _____
   Notes: _____
World History/Geography: _____
   Notes: _____
Foreign Language: _____
   Notes: _____
Sports/Fitness/Phys. Ed.: _____
   Notes: _____
Music: _____
   Notes: _____
Visual Arts: _____
   Notes: _____
Performing Arts: _____
   Notes: _____
Religious/Cultural Studies: _____
   Notes: _____
Field Trips: _____
   Notes: _____
Trade Skills/Shop: _____
   Notes: _____
Health/Hygiene/Nutrition: _____
   Notes: _____
Computers/Tech./Business Skills: _____
   Notes: _____
Comm. Svc./Volunteerism/Career: _____
   Notes: _____
Home Economics/Chores: _____
   Notes: _____
Electives/Hobbies/Clubs: _____
   Notes: _____
Miscellaneous: _____

Day 150   Date: __ /__ /__   Hours: _____   Admin. Notes: _____

Reading/Literature: _____
  Notes: _____

Writing/Language Arts: _____
  Notes: _____

Mathematics: _____
  Notes: _____

Science/Lab: _____
  Notes: _____

US Hist./Govt./Civics: _____
  Notes: _____

World History/Geography: _____
  Notes: _____

Foreign Language: _____
  Notes: _____

Sports/Fitness/Phys. Ed.: _____
  Notes: _____

Music: _____
  Notes: _____

Visual Arts: _____
  Notes: _____

Performing Arts: _____
  Notes: _____

Religious/Cultural Studies: _____
  Notes: _____

Field Trips: _____
  Notes: _____

Trade Skills/Shop: _____
  Notes: _____

Health/Hygiene/Nutrition: _____
  Notes: _____

Computers/Tech./Business Skills: _____
  Notes: _____

Comm. Svc./Volunteerism/Career: _____
  Notes: _____

Home Economics/Chores: _____
  Notes: _____

Electives/Hobbies/Clubs: _____
  Notes: _____

Miscellaneous: _____
_____

Day 151 Date: __ /__ /__ Hours: _____ Admin. Notes: _____

Reading/Literature: _____
   Notes: _____
Writing/Language Arts: _____
   Notes: _____
Mathematics: _____
   Notes: _____
Science/Lab: _____
   Notes: _____
US Hist./Govt./Civics: _____
   Notes: _____
World History/Geography: _____
   Notes: _____
Foreign Language: _____
   Notes: _____
Sports/Fitness/Phys. Ed.: _____
   Notes: _____
Music: _____
   Notes: _____
Visual Arts: _____
   Notes: _____
Performing Arts: _____
   Notes: _____
Religious/Cultural Studies: _____
   Notes: _____
Field Trips: _____
   Notes: _____
Trade Skills/Shop: _____
   Notes: _____
Health/Hygiene/Nutrition: _____
   Notes: _____
Computers/Tech./Business Skills: _____
   Notes: _____
Comm. Svc./Volunteerism/Career: _____
   Notes: _____
Home Economics/Chores: _____
   Notes: _____
Electives/Hobbies/Clubs: _____
   Notes: _____
Miscellaneous: _____

Day 152   Date: __ /__ /__   Hours: _____   Admin. Notes: _____

Reading/Literature: _____
  Notes: _____
Writing/Language Arts: _____
  Notes: _____
Mathematics: _____
  Notes: _____
Science/Lab: _____
  Notes: _____
US Hist./Govt./Civics: _____
  Notes: _____
World History/Geography: _____
  Notes: _____
Foreign Language: _____
  Notes: _____
Sports/Fitness/Phys. Ed.: _____
  Notes: _____
Music: _____
  Notes: _____
Visual Arts: _____
  Notes: _____
Performing Arts: _____
  Notes: _____
Religious/Cultural Studies: _____
  Notes: _____
Field Trips: _____
  Notes: _____
Trade Skills/Shop: _____
  Notes: _____
Health/Hygiene/Nutrition: _____
  Notes: _____
Computers/Tech./Business Skills: _____
  Notes: _____
Comm. Svc./Volunteerism/Career: _____
  Notes: _____
Home Economics/Chores: _____
  Notes: _____
Electives/Hobbies/Clubs: _____
  Notes: _____
Miscellaneous: _____

Day 153 Date: __ /__ /__ Hours: _____ Admin. Notes: _____

Reading/Literature: _____
 Notes: _____
Writing/Language Arts: _____
 Notes: _____
Mathematics: _____
 Notes: _____
Science/Lab: _____
 Notes: _____
US Hist./Govt./Civics: _____
 Notes: _____
World History/Geography: _____
 Notes: _____
Foreign Language: _____
 Notes: _____
Sports/Fitness/Phys. Ed.: _____
 Notes: _____
Music: _____
 Notes: _____
Visual Arts: _____
 Notes: _____
Performing Arts: _____
 Notes: _____
Religious/Cultural Studies: _____
 Notes: _____
Field Trips: _____
 Notes: _____
Trade Skills/Shop: _____
 Notes: _____
Health/Hygiene/Nutrition: _____
 Notes: _____
Computers/Tech./Business Skills: _____
 Notes: _____
Comm. Svc./Volunteerism/Career: _____
 Notes: _____
Home Economics/Chores: _____
 Notes: _____
Electives/Hobbies/Clubs: _____
 Notes: _____
Miscellaneous: _____

Day 154   Date: __ / __ / __   Hours: _____   Admin. Notes: _____

Reading/Literature: _____
  Notes: _____
Writing/Language Arts: _____
  Notes: _____
Mathematics: _____
  Notes: _____
Science/Lab: _____
  Notes: _____
US Hist./Govt./Civics: _____
  Notes: _____
World History/Geography: _____
  Notes: _____
Foreign Language: _____
  Notes: _____
Sports/Fitness/Phys. Ed.: _____
  Notes: _____
Music: _____
  Notes: _____
Visual Arts: _____
  Notes: _____
Performing Arts: _____
  Notes: _____
Religious/Cultural Studies: _____
  Notes: _____
Field Trips: _____
  Notes: _____
Trade Skills/Shop: _____
  Notes: _____
Health/Hygiene/Nutrition: _____
  Notes: _____
Computers/Tech./Business Skills: _____
  Notes: _____
Comm. Svc./Volunteerism/Career: _____
  Notes: _____
Home Economics/Chores: _____
  Notes: _____
Electives/Hobbies/Clubs: _____
  Notes: _____
Miscellaneous: _____

Day 155   Date: __ /__ /__   Hours: _____   Admin. Notes: _____

Reading/Literature: _____
  Notes: _____
Writing/Language Arts: _____
  Notes: _____
Mathematics: _____
  Notes: _____
Science/Lab: _____
  Notes: _____
US Hist./Govt./Civics: _____
  Notes: _____
World History/Geography: _____
  Notes: _____
Foreign Language: _____
  Notes: _____
Sports/Fitness/Phys. Ed.: _____
  Notes: _____
Music: _____
  Notes: _____
Visual Arts: _____
  Notes: _____
Performing Arts: _____
  Notes: _____
Religious/Cultural Studies: _____
  Notes: _____
Field Trips: _____
  Notes: _____
Trade Skills/Shop: _____
  Notes: _____
Health/Hygiene/Nutrition: _____
  Notes: _____
Computers/Tech./Business Skills: _____
  Notes: _____
Comm. Svc./Volunteerism/Career: _____
  Notes: _____
Home Economics/Chores: _____
  Notes: _____
Electives/Hobbies/Clubs: _____
  Notes: _____
Miscellaneous: _____

Day 156   Date: __ /__ /__ Hours: _____ Admin. Notes: _____

Reading/Literature: _____
   Notes: _____

Writing/Language Arts: _____
   Notes: _____

Mathematics: _____
   Notes: _____

Science/Lab: _____
   Notes: _____

US Hist./Govt./Civics: _____
   Notes: _____

World History/Geography: _____
   Notes: _____

Foreign Language: _____
   Notes: _____

Sports/Fitness/Phys. Ed.: _____
   Notes: _____

Music: _____
   Notes: _____

Visual Arts: _____
   Notes: _____

Performing Arts: _____
   Notes: _____

Religious/Cultural Studies: _____
   Notes: _____

Field Trips: _____
   Notes: _____

Trade Skills/Shop: _____
   Notes: _____

Health/Hygiene/Nutrition: _____
   Notes: _____

Computers/Tech./Business Skills: _____
   Notes: _____

Comm. Svc./Volunteerism/Career: _____
   Notes: _____

Home Economics/Chores: _____
   Notes: _____

Electives/Hobbies/Clubs: _____
   Notes: _____

Miscellaneous: _____

Day 157 Date: __ / __ / __ Hours: _____ Admin. Notes: _____

Reading/Literature: _____
  Notes: _____

Writing/Language Arts: _____
  Notes: _____

Mathematics: _____
  Notes: _____

Science/Lab: _____
  Notes: _____

US Hist./Govt./Civics: _____
  Notes: _____

World History/Geography: _____
  Notes: _____

Foreign Language: _____
  Notes: _____

Sports/Fitness/Phys. Ed.: _____
  Notes: _____

Music: _____
  Notes: _____

Visual Arts: _____
  Notes: _____

Performing Arts: _____
  Notes: _____

Religious/Cultural Studies: _____
  Notes: _____

Field Trips: _____
  Notes: _____

Trade Skills/Shop: _____
  Notes: _____

Health/Hygiene/Nutrition: _____
  Notes: _____

Computers/Tech./Business Skills: _____
  Notes: _____

Comm. Svc./Volunteerism/Career: _____
  Notes: _____

Home Economics/Chores: _____
  Notes: _____

Electives/Hobbies/Clubs: _____
  Notes: _____

Miscellaneous: _____

Day 158 Date: __ / __ / __ Hours: _____ Admin. Notes: _____

Reading/Literature: _____
   Notes: _____

Writing/Language Arts: _____
   Notes: _____

Mathematics: _____
   Notes: _____

Science/Lab: _____
   Notes: _____

US Hist./Govt./Civics: _____
   Notes: _____

World History/Geography: _____
   Notes: _____

Foreign Language: _____
   Notes: _____

Sports/Fitness/Phys. Ed.: _____
   Notes: _____

Music: _____
   Notes: _____

Visual Arts: _____
   Notes: _____

Performing Arts: _____
   Notes: _____

Religious/Cultural Studies: _____
   Notes: _____

Field Trips: _____
   Notes: _____

Trade Skills/Shop: _____
   Notes: _____

Health/Hygiene/Nutrition: _____
   Notes: _____

Computers/Tech./Business Skills: _____
   Notes: _____

Comm. Svc./Volunteerism/Career: _____
   Notes: _____

Home Economics/Chores: _____
   Notes: _____

Electives/Hobbies/Clubs: _____
   Notes: _____

Miscellaneous: _____
_____

Day 159   Date: __ /__ /__   Hours: _____   Admin. Notes: _____

Reading/Literature: _____
　Notes: _____
Writing/Language Arts: _____
　Notes: _____
Mathematics: _____
　Notes: _____
Science/Lab: _____
　Notes: _____
US Hist./Govt./Civics: _____
　Notes: _____
World History/Geography: _____
　Notes: _____
Foreign Language: _____
　Notes: _____
Sports/Fitness/Phys. Ed.: _____
　Notes: _____
Music: _____
　Notes: _____
Visual Arts: _____
　Notes: _____
Performing Arts: _____
　Notes: _____
Religious/Cultural Studies: _____
　Notes: _____
Field Trips: _____
　Notes: _____
Trade Skills/Shop: _____
　Notes: _____
Health/Hygiene/Nutrition: _____
　Notes: _____
Computers/Tech./Business Skills: _____
　Notes: _____
Comm. Svc./Volunteerism/Career: _____
　Notes: _____
Home Economics/Chores: _____
　Notes: _____
Electives/Hobbies/Clubs: _____
　Notes: _____
Miscellaneous: _____
_____

Day 160   Date: __ /__ /__   Hours: _____   Admin. Notes: _____

Reading/Literature: _____
   Notes: _____

Writing/Language Arts: _____
   Notes: _____

Mathematics: _____
   Notes: _____

Science/Lab: _____
   Notes: _____

US Hist./Govt./Civics: _____
   Notes: _____

World History/Geography: _____
   Notes: _____

Foreign Language: _____
   Notes: _____

Sports/Fitness/Phys. Ed.: _____
   Notes: _____

Music: _____
   Notes: _____

Visual Arts: _____
   Notes: _____

Performing Arts: _____
   Notes: _____

Religious/Cultural Studies: _____
   Notes: _____

Field Trips: _____
   Notes: _____

Trade Skills/Shop: _____
   Notes: _____

Health/Hygiene/Nutrition: _____
   Notes: _____

Computers/Tech./Business Skills: _____
   Notes: _____

Comm. Svc./Volunteerism/Career: _____
   Notes: _____

Home Economics/Chores: _____
   Notes: _____

Electives/Hobbies/Clubs: _____
   Notes: _____

Miscellaneous: _____

Day 161 Date: __ /__ /__ Hours: _____ Admin. Notes:_____

Reading/Literature: _____
Notes: _____
Writing/Language Arts: _____
Notes: _____
Mathematics: _____
Notes: _____
Science/Lab: _____
Notes: _____
US Hist./Govt./Civics: _____
Notes: _____
World History/Geography: _____
Notes: _____
Foreign Language: _____
Notes: _____
Sports/Fitness/Phys. Ed.: _____
Notes: _____
Music: _____
Notes: _____
Visual Arts: _____
Notes: _____
Performing Arts: _____
Notes: _____
Religious/Cultural Studies: _____
Notes: _____
Field Trips: _____
Notes: _____
Trade Skills/Shop: _____
Notes: _____
Health/Hygiene/Nutrition: _____
Notes: _____
Computers/Tech./Business Skills: _____
Notes: _____
Comm. Svc./Volunteerism/Career: _____
Notes: _____
Home Economics/Chores: _____
Notes: _____
Electives/Hobbies/Clubs: _____
Notes: _____
Miscellaneous: _____

Day 162 Date: __ / __ / __ Hours: _____ Admin. Notes: _____

Reading/Literature: _____
Notes: _____

Writing/Language Arts: _____
Notes: _____

Mathematics: _____
Notes: _____

Science/Lab: _____
Notes: _____

US Hist./Govt./Civics: _____
Notes: _____

World History/Geography: _____
Notes: _____

Foreign Language: _____
Notes: _____

Sports/Fitness/Phys. Ed.: _____
Notes: _____

Music: _____
Notes: _____

Visual Arts: _____
Notes: _____

Performing Arts: _____
Notes: _____

Religious/Cultural Studies: _____
Notes: _____

Field Trips: _____
Notes: _____

Trade Skills/Shop: _____
Notes: _____

Health/Hygiene/Nutrition: _____
Notes: _____

Computers/Tech./Business Skills: _____
Notes: _____

Comm. Svc./Volunteerism/Career: _____
Notes: _____

Home Economics/Chores: _____
Notes: _____

Electives/Hobbies/Clubs: _____
Notes: _____

Miscellaneous: _____

Day 163 Date: __ /__ /__ Hours: _____ Admin. Notes: _____

Reading/Literature: _____
  Notes: _____
Writing/Language Arts: _____
  Notes: _____
Mathematics: _____
  Notes: _____
Science/Lab: _____
  Notes: _____
US Hist./Govt./Civics: _____
  Notes: _____
World History/Geography: _____
  Notes: _____
Foreign Language: _____
  Notes: _____
Sports/Fitness/Phys. Ed.: _____
  Notes: _____
Music: _____
  Notes: _____
Visual Arts: _____
  Notes: _____
Performing Arts: _____
  Notes: _____
Religious/Cultural Studies: _____
  Notes: _____
Field Trips: _____
  Notes: _____
Trade Skills/Shop: _____
  Notes: _____
Health/Hygiene/Nutrition: _____
  Notes: _____
Computers/Tech./Business Skills: _____
  Notes: _____
Comm. Svc./Volunteerism/Career: _____
  Notes: _____
Home Economics/Chores: _____
  Notes: _____
Electives/Hobbies/Clubs: _____
  Notes: _____
Miscellaneous: _____

Day 164   Date: __ /__ /__   Hours: _____   Admin. Notes: _____

Reading/Literature: _____
   Notes: _____
Writing/Language Arts: _____
   Notes: _____
Mathematics: _____
   Notes: _____
Science/Lab: _____
   Notes: _____
US Hist./Govt./Civics: _____
   Notes: _____
World History/Geography: _____
   Notes: _____
Foreign Language: _____
   Notes: _____
Sports/Fitness/Phys. Ed.: _____
   Notes: _____
Music: _____
   Notes: _____
Visual Arts: _____
   Notes: _____
Performing Arts: _____
   Notes: _____
Religious/Cultural Studies: _____
   Notes: _____
Field Trips: _____
   Notes: _____
Trade Skills/Shop: _____
   Notes: _____
Health/Hygiene/Nutrition: _____
   Notes: _____
Computers/Tech./Business Skills: _____
   Notes: _____
Comm. Svc./Volunteerism/Career: _____
   Notes: _____
Home Economics/Chores: _____
   Notes: _____
Electives/Hobbies/Clubs: _____
   Notes: _____
Miscellaneous: _____

Day 165   Date: __ /__ /__   Hours: _____   Admin. Notes:_____

Reading/Literature: _____
  Notes: _____
Writing/Language Arts: _____
  Notes: _____
Mathematics: _____
  Notes: _____
Science/Lab: _____
  Notes: _____
US Hist./Govt./Civics:_____
  Notes: _____
World History/Geography: _____
  Notes: _____
Foreign Language: _____
  Notes: _____
Sports/Fitness/Phys. Ed.: _____
  Notes: _____
Music: _____
  Notes: _____
Visual Arts: _____
  Notes: _____
Performing Arts: _____
  Notes: _____
Religious/Cultural Studies: _____
  Notes: _____
Field Trips: _____
  Notes: _____
Trade Skills/Shop:_____
  Notes: _____
Health/Hygiene/Nutrition: _____
  Notes: _____
Computers/Tech./Business Skills: _____
  Notes: _____
Comm. Svc./Volunteerism/Career:_____
  Notes: _____
Home Economics/Chores: _____
  Notes: _____
Electives/Hobbies/Clubs: _____
  Notes: _____
Miscellaneous: _____

Day 166 Date: __ / __ / __ Hours: _____ Admin. Notes: _____

Reading/Literature: _____
   Notes: _____
Writing/Language Arts: _____
   Notes: _____
Mathematics: _____
   Notes: _____
Science/Lab: _____
   Notes: _____
US Hist./Govt./Civics: _____
   Notes: _____
World History/Geography: _____
   Notes: _____
Foreign Language: _____
   Notes: _____
Sports/Fitness/Phys. Ed.: _____
   Notes: _____
Music: _____
   Notes: _____
Visual Arts: _____
   Notes: _____
Performing Arts: _____
   Notes: _____
Religious/Cultural Studies: _____
   Notes: _____
Field Trips: _____
   Notes: _____
Trade Skills/Shop: _____
   Notes: _____
Health/Hygiene/Nutrition: _____
   Notes: _____
Computers/Tech./Business Skills: _____
   Notes: _____
Comm. Svc./Volunteerism/Career: _____
   Notes: _____
Home Economics/Chores: _____
   Notes: _____
Electives/Hobbies/Clubs: _____
   Notes: _____
Miscellaneous: _____
_____

Day 167 Date: __ /__ /__ Hours: _____ Admin. Notes: _____

Reading/Literature: _____
Notes: _____
Writing/Language Arts: _____
Notes: _____
Mathematics: _____
Notes: _____
Science/Lab: _____
Notes: _____
US Hist./Govt./Civics: _____
Notes: _____
World History/Geography: _____
Notes: _____
Foreign Language: _____
Notes: _____
Sports/Fitness/Phys. Ed.: _____
Notes: _____
Music: _____
Notes: _____
Visual Arts: _____
Notes: _____
Performing Arts: _____
Notes: _____
Religious/Cultural Studies: _____
Notes: _____
Field Trips: _____
Notes: _____
Trade Skills/Shop: _____
Notes: _____
Health/Hygiene/Nutrition: _____
Notes: _____
Computers/Tech./Business Skills: _____
Notes: _____
Comm. Svc./Volunteerism/Career: _____
Notes: _____
Home Economics/Chores: _____
Notes: _____
Electives/Hobbies/Clubs: _____
Notes: _____
Miscellaneous: _____

Day 168   Date: __ /__ /__   Hours: _____   Admin. Notes: _____

Reading/Literature: _____
Notes: _____

Writing/Language Arts: _____
Notes: _____

Mathematics: _____
Notes: _____

Science/Lab: _____
Notes: _____

US Hist./Govt./Civics: _____
Notes: _____

World History/Geography: _____
Notes: _____

Foreign Language: _____
Notes: _____

Sports/Fitness/Phys. Ed.: _____
Notes: _____

Music: _____
Notes: _____

Visual Arts: _____
Notes: _____

Performing Arts: _____
Notes: _____

Religious/Cultural Studies: _____
Notes: _____

Field Trips: _____
Notes: _____

Trade Skills/Shop: _____
Notes: _____

Health/Hygiene/Nutrition: _____
Notes: _____

Computers/Tech./Business Skills: _____
Notes: _____

Comm. Svc./Volunteerism/Career: _____
Notes: _____

Home Economics/Chores: _____
Notes: _____

Electives/Hobbies/Clubs: _____
Notes: _____

Miscellaneous: _____

_____

Day 169 Date: __ /__ /__ Hours: _____ Admin. Notes:_____

Reading/Literature: _____
  Notes: _____
Writing/Language Arts: _____
  Notes: _____
Mathematics: _____
  Notes: _____
Science/Lab: _____
  Notes: _____
US Hist./Govt./Civics: _____
  Notes: _____
World History/Geography: _____
  Notes: _____
Foreign Language: _____
  Notes: _____
Sports/Fitness/Phys. Ed.: _____
  Notes: _____
Music: _____
  Notes: _____
Visual Arts: _____
  Notes: _____
Performing Arts: _____
  Notes: _____
Religious/Cultural Studies: _____
  Notes: _____
Field Trips: _____
  Notes: _____
Trade Skills/Shop: _____
  Notes: _____
Health/Hygiene/Nutrition: _____
  Notes: _____
Computers/Tech./Business Skills: _____
  Notes: _____
Comm. Svc./Volunteerism/Career: _____
  Notes: _____
Home Economics/Chores: _____
  Notes: _____
Electives/Hobbies/Clubs: _____
  Notes: _____
Miscellaneous: _____
_____

Day 170 Date: __ / __ / __ Hours: _____ Admin. Notes: _____

Reading/Literature: _____
   Notes: _____

Writing/Language Arts: _____
   Notes: _____

Mathematics: _____
   Notes: _____

Science/Lab: _____
   Notes: _____

US Hist./Govt./Civics: _____
   Notes: _____

World History/Geography: _____
   Notes: _____

Foreign Language: _____
   Notes: _____

Sports/Fitness/Phys. Ed.: _____
   Notes: _____

Music: _____
   Notes: _____

Visual Arts: _____
   Notes: _____

Performing Arts: _____
   Notes: _____

Religious/Cultural Studies: _____
   Notes: _____

Field Trips: _____
   Notes: _____

Trade Skills/Shop: _____
   Notes: _____

Health/Hygiene/Nutrition: _____
   Notes: _____

Computers/Tech./Business Skills: _____
   Notes: _____

Comm. Svc./Volunteerism/Career: _____
   Notes: _____

Home Economics/Chores: _____
   Notes: _____

Electives/Hobbies/Clubs: _____
   Notes: _____

Miscellaneous: _____

Day 171   Date: __ /__ /__   Hours: _____   Admin. Notes: _____

Reading/Literature: _____
   Notes: _____
Writing/Language Arts: _____
   Notes: _____
Mathematics: _____
   Notes: _____
Science/Lab: _____
   Notes: _____
US Hist./Govt./Civics: _____
   Notes: _____
World History/Geography: _____
   Notes: _____
Foreign Language: _____
   Notes: _____
Sports/Fitness/Phys. Ed.: _____
   Notes: _____
Music: _____
   Notes: _____
Visual Arts: _____
   Notes: _____
Performing Arts: _____
   Notes: _____
Religious/Cultural Studies: _____
   Notes: _____
Field Trips: _____
   Notes: _____
Trade Skills/Shop: _____
   Notes: _____
Health/Hygiene/Nutrition: _____
   Notes: _____
Computers/Tech./Business Skills: _____
   Notes: _____
Comm. Svc./Volunteerism/Career: _____
   Notes: _____
Home Economics/Chores: _____
   Notes: _____
Electives/Hobbies/Clubs: _____
   Notes: _____
Miscellaneous: _____
_____

Day 172   Date: __ /__ /__   Hours: _____   Admin. Notes: _____

Reading/Literature: _____
  Notes: _____
Writing/Language Arts: _____
  Notes: _____
Mathematics: _____
  Notes: _____
Science/Lab: _____
  Notes: _____
US Hist./Govt./Civics: _____
  Notes: _____
World History/Geography: _____
  Notes: _____
Foreign Language: _____
  Notes: _____
Sports/Fitness/Phys. Ed.: _____
  Notes: _____
Music: _____
  Notes: _____
Visual Arts: _____
  Notes: _____
Performing Arts: _____
  Notes: _____
Religious/Cultural Studies: _____
  Notes: _____
Field Trips: _____
  Notes: _____
Trade Skills/Shop: _____
  Notes: _____
Health/Hygiene/Nutrition: _____
  Notes: _____
Computers/Tech./Business Skills: _____
  Notes: _____
Comm. Svc./Volunteerism/Career: _____
  Notes: _____
Home Economics/Chores: _____
  Notes: _____
Electives/Hobbies/Clubs: _____
  Notes: _____
Miscellaneous: _____

Day 173 Date: __ /__ /__ Hours: _____ Admin. Notes:_____

Reading/Literature: _____
Notes: _____

Writing/Language Arts: _____
Notes: _____

Mathematics: _____
Notes: _____

Science/Lab: _____
Notes: _____

US Hist./Govt./Civics: _____
Notes: _____

World History/Geography: _____
Notes: _____

Foreign Language: _____
Notes: _____

Sports/Fitness/Phys. Ed.: _____
Notes: _____

Music: _____
Notes: _____

Visual Arts: _____
Notes: _____

Performing Arts: _____
Notes: _____

Religious/Cultural Studies: _____
Notes: _____

Field Trips: _____
Notes: _____

Trade Skills/Shop: _____
Notes: _____

Health/Hygiene/Nutrition: _____
Notes: _____

Computers/Tech./Business Skills: _____
Notes: _____

Comm. Svc./Volunteerism/Career: _____
Notes: _____

Home Economics/Chores: _____
Notes: _____

Electives/Hobbies/Clubs: _____
Notes: _____

Miscellaneous: _____

Day 174   Date: __ /__ /__   Hours: _____   Admin. Notes: _____

Reading/Literature: _____
  Notes: _____
Writing/Language Arts: _____
  Notes: _____
Mathematics: _____
  Notes: _____
Science/Lab: _____
  Notes: _____
US Hist./Govt./Civics: _____
  Notes: _____
World History/Geography: _____
  Notes: _____
Foreign Language: _____
  Notes: _____
Sports/Fitness/Phys. Ed.: _____
  Notes: _____
Music: _____
  Notes: _____
Visual Arts: _____
  Notes: _____
Performing Arts: _____
  Notes: _____
Religious/Cultural Studies: _____
  Notes: _____
Field Trips: _____
  Notes: _____
Trade Skills/Shop: _____
  Notes: _____
Health/Hygiene/Nutrition: _____
  Notes: _____
Computers/Tech./Business Skills: _____
  Notes: _____
Comm. Svc./Volunteerism/Career: _____
  Notes: _____
Home Economics/Chores: _____
  Notes: _____
Electives/Hobbies/Clubs: _____
  Notes: _____
Miscellaneous: _____
_____

Day 175   Date: __ /__ /__   Hours: _____   Admin. Notes: _____

Reading/Literature: _____
  Notes: _____
Writing/Language Arts: _____
  Notes: _____
Mathematics: _____
  Notes: _____
Science/Lab: _____
  Notes: _____
US Hist./Govt./Civics: _____
  Notes: _____
World History/Geography: _____
  Notes: _____
Foreign Language: _____
  Notes: _____
Sports/Fitness/Phys. Ed.: _____
  Notes: _____
Music: _____
  Notes: _____
Visual Arts: _____
  Notes: _____
Performing Arts: _____
  Notes: _____
Religious/Cultural Studies: _____
  Notes: _____
Field Trips: _____
  Notes: _____
Trade Skills/Shop: _____
  Notes: _____
Health/Hygiene/Nutrition: _____
  Notes: _____
Computers/Tech./Business Skills: _____
  Notes: _____
Comm. Svc./Volunteerism/Career: _____
  Notes: _____
Home Economics/Chores: _____
  Notes: _____
Electives/Hobbies/Clubs: _____
  Notes: _____
Miscellaneous: _____
_____

Day 176 Date: __ /__ /__ Hours: _____ Admin. Notes: _____

Reading/Literature: _____
  Notes: _____

Writing/Language Arts: _____
  Notes: _____

Mathematics: _____
  Notes: _____

Science/Lab: _____
  Notes: _____

US Hist./Govt./Civics: _____
  Notes: _____

World History/Geography: _____
  Notes: _____

Foreign Language: _____
  Notes: _____

Sports/Fitness/Phys. Ed.: _____
  Notes: _____

Music: _____
  Notes: _____

Visual Arts: _____
  Notes: _____

Performing Arts: _____
  Notes: _____

Religious/Cultural Studies: _____
  Notes: _____

Field Trips: _____
  Notes: _____

Trade Skills/Shop: _____
  Notes: _____

Health/Hygiene/Nutrition: _____
  Notes: _____

Computers/Tech./Business Skills: _____
  Notes: _____

Comm. Svc./Volunteerism/Career: _____
  Notes: _____

Home Economics/Chores: _____
  Notes: _____

Electives/Hobbies/Clubs: _____
  Notes: _____

Miscellaneous: _____

Day 177 Date: __ /__ /__ Hours: _____ Admin. Notes:_____

Reading/Literature: _____
Notes: _____
Writing/Language Arts: _____
Notes: _____
Mathematics: _____
Notes: _____
Science/Lab: _____
Notes: _____
US Hist./Govt./Civics:_____
Notes: _____
World History/Geography: _____
Notes: _____
Foreign Language:_____
Notes: _____
Sports/Fitness/Phys. Ed.: _____
Notes: _____
Music: _____
Notes: _____
Visual Arts: _____
Notes: _____
Performing Arts: _____
Notes: _____
Religious/Cultural Studies: _____
Notes: _____
Field Trips: _____
Notes: _____
Trade Skills/Shop:_____
Notes: _____
Health/Hygiene/Nutrition: _____
Notes: _____
Computers/Tech./Business Skills: _____
Notes: _____
Comm. Svc./Volunteerism/Career:_____
Notes: _____
Home Economics/Chores: _____
Notes: _____
Electives/Hobbies/Clubs:_____
Notes: _____
Miscellaneous: _____
_____

Day 178   Date: __ /__ /__   Hours: _____   Admin. Notes: _____

Reading/Literature: _____
Notes: _____
Writing/Language Arts: _____
Notes: _____
Mathematics: _____
Notes: _____
Science/Lab: _____
Notes: _____
US Hist./Govt./Civics: _____
Notes: _____
World History/Geography: _____
Notes: _____
Foreign Language: _____
Notes: _____
Sports/Fitness/Phys. Ed.: _____
Notes: _____
Music: _____
Notes: _____
Visual Arts: _____
Notes: _____
Performing Arts: _____
Notes: _____
Religious/Cultural Studies: _____
Notes: _____
Field Trips: _____
Notes: _____
Trade Skills/Shop: _____
Notes: _____
Health/Hygiene/Nutrition: _____
Notes: _____
Computers/Tech./Business Skills: _____
Notes: _____
Comm. Svc./Volunteerism/Career: _____
Notes: _____
Home Economics/Chores: _____
Notes: _____
Electives/Hobbies/Clubs: _____
Notes: _____
Miscellaneous: _____

Day 179 Date: __ /__ /__ Hours: _____ Admin. Notes: _____

Reading/Literature: _____
  Notes: _____
Writing/Language Arts: _____
  Notes: _____
Mathematics: _____
  Notes: _____
Science/Lab: _____
  Notes: _____
US Hist./Govt./Civics: _____
  Notes: _____
World History/Geography: _____
  Notes: _____
Foreign Language: _____
  Notes: _____
Sports/Fitness/Phys. Ed.: _____
  Notes: _____
Music: _____
  Notes: _____
Visual Arts: _____
  Notes: _____
Performing Arts: _____
  Notes: _____
Religious/Cultural Studies: _____
  Notes: _____
Field Trips: _____
  Notes: _____
Trade Skills/Shop: _____
  Notes: _____
Health/Hygiene/Nutrition: _____
  Notes: _____
Computers/Tech./Business Skills: _____
  Notes: _____
Comm. Svc./Volunteerism/Career: _____
  Notes: _____
Home Economics/Chores: _____
  Notes: _____
Electives/Hobbies/Clubs: _____
  Notes: _____
Miscellaneous: _____

Made in United States
Orlando, FL
14 June 2022

18808565R00104

Day 180   Date: __ /__ /__   Hours: _____   Admin. Notes: _____

Reading/Literature: _____
   Notes: _____

Writing/Language Arts: _____
   Notes: _____

Mathematics: _____
   Notes: _____

Science/Lab: _____
   Notes: _____

US Hist./Govt./Civics: _____
   Notes: _____

World History/Geography: _____
   Notes: _____

Foreign Language: _____
   Notes: _____

Sports/Fitness/Phys. Ed.: _____
   Notes: _____

Music: _____
   Notes: _____

Visual Arts: _____
   Notes: _____

Performing Arts: _____
   Notes: _____

Religious/Cultural Studies: _____
   Notes: _____

Field Trips: _____
   Notes: _____

Trade Skills/Shop: _____
   Notes: _____

Health/Hygiene/Nutrition: _____
   Notes: _____

Computers/Tech./Business Skills: _____
   Notes: _____

Comm. Svc./Volunteerism/Career: _____
   Notes: _____

Home Economics/Chores: _____
   Notes: _____

Electives/Hobbies/Clubs: _____
   Notes: _____

Miscellaneous: _____